Liquidity and Asset Prices

Liquidity and Asset Prices

Yakov Amihud

Ira Leon Rennert Professor of Finance
Stern School of Business
New York University
yamihud@stern.nyu.edu

Haim Mendelson

The Kleiner, Perkins, Caufield &
Byers Professor of Electronic Business
and Commerce, and Management
Graduate School of Business
Stanford University

Lasse Heje Pedersen

Charles Schaefer Associate Professor of Finance
Stern School of Business
New York University

the essence of knowledge

Boston – Delft

Foundations and Trends® in Finance

Published, sold and distributed by:
now Publishers Inc.
PO Box 1024
Hanover, MA 02339
USA
Tel. +1-781-985-4510
www.nowpublishers.com
sales@nowpublishers.com

Outside North America:
now Publishers Inc.
PO Box 179
2600 AD Delft
The Netherlands
Tel. +31-6-51115274

A Cataloging-in-Publication record is available from the Library of Congress

The preferred citation for this publication is Y. Amihud, H. Mendelson, and L.H. Pedersen, Liquidity and Asset Prices, Foundation and Trends® in Finance, vol 1, no 4, pp 269–364, 2005

Printed on acid-free paper

ISBN: 1-933019-12-3
© 2006 Y. Amihud, H. Mendelson, and L.H. Pedersen

All rights reserved. No part of this publication may be reproduced, stored in a retrieval system, or transmitted in any form or by any means, mechanical, photocopying, recording or otherwise, without prior written permission of the publishers.

Photocopying. In the USA: This journal is registered at the Copyright Clearance Center, Inc., 222 Rosewood Drive, Danvers, MA 01923. Authorization to photocopy items for internal or personal use, or the internal or personal use of specific clients, is granted by now Publishers Inc for users registered with the Copyright Clearance Center (CCC). The 'services' for users can be found on the internet at: www.copyright.com

For those organizations that have been granted a photocopy license, a separate system of payment has been arranged. Authorization does not extend to other kinds of copying, such as that for general distribution, for advertising or promotional purposes, for creating new collective works, or for resale. In the rest of the world: Permission to photocopy must be obtained from the copyright owner. Please apply to now Publishers Inc., PO Box 1024, Hanover, MA 02339, USA; Tel. +1 781 871 0245; www.nowpublishers.com; sales@nowpublishers.com

now Publishers Inc. has an exclusive license to publish this material worldwide. Permission to use this content must be obtained from the copyright license holder. Please apply to now Publishers, PO Box 179, 2600 AD Delft, The Netherlands, www.nowpublishers.com; e-mail: sales@nowpublishers.com

Foundations and Trends® in Finance
Volume 1 Issue 4, 2005
Editorial Board

Editor-in-Chief:
George M. Constantinides
Leo Melamed Professor of Finance
The University of Chicago
Graduate School of Business
5807 South Woodlawn Avenue
Chicago IL 60637
USA
gmc@gsb.uchicago.edu

Editors

Franklin Allen
The University of Pennsylvania

Andrew W. Lo
Massachusetts Institute of Technology

René M. Stulz
The Ohio State University

Editorial Scope

Foundations and Trends® in Finance will publish survey and tutorial articles in the following topics:

- Corporate Governance
- Corporate Financing
- Dividend Policy and Capital Structure
- Corporate Control
- Investment Policy
- Agency Theory and Information
- Market Microstructure
- Portfolio Theory
- Financial Intermediation
- Investment Banking
- Market Efficiency
- Security Issuance
- Anomalies and Behavioral Finance
- Asset-Pricing Theory
- Asset-Pricing Models
- Tax Effects
- Liquidity
- Equity Risk Premium
- Pricing Models and Volatility
- Fixed Income Securities
- Computational Finance
- Futures Markets and Hedging
- Financial Engineering
- Interest Rate Derivatives
- Credit Derivatives
- Financial Econometrics
- Estimating Volatilities and Correlations

Information for Librarians

Foundations and Trends® in Finance, 2005, Volume 1, 4 issues. ISSN paper version 1567-2395. ISSN online version 1567-2409. Also available as a combined paper and online subscription.

Foundations and Trends® in
Finance
Vol. 1, No 4 (2005) 269–364
© 2006 Y. Amihud, H. Mendelson, and L.H. Pedersen

Liquidity and Asset Prices

Yakov Amihud[1], Haim Mendelson[2] and Lasse Heje Pedersen[3]

[1] Stern School of Business, New York University, yamihud@stern.nyu.edu
[2] Graduate School of Business, Stanford University
[3] Stern School of Business, New York University

Abstract

We review the theories on how liquidity affects the required returns of capital assets and the empirical studies that test these theories. The theory predicts that both the level of liquidity and liquidity risk are priced, and empirical studies find the effects of liquidity on asset prices to be statistically significant and economically important, controlling for traditional risk measures and asset characteristics. Liquidity-based asset pricing empirically helps explain (1) the cross-section of stock returns, (2) how a reduction in stock liquidity result in a reduction in stock prices and an increase in expected stock returns, (3) the yield differential between on- and off-the-run Treasuries, (4) the yield spreads on corporate bonds, (5) the returns on hedge funds, (6) the valuation of closed-end funds, and (7) the low price of certain hard-to-trade securities relative to more liquid counterparts with identical cash flows, such as restricted stocks or illiquid derivatives. Liquidity can thus play a role in resolving a number of asset pricing puzzles such as the small-firm effect, the equity premium puzzle, and the risk-free rate puzzle.

Contents

1 Introduction   1

2 Theory   5

2.1 Liquidity and standard asset pricing theory   5
2.2 Basic model of liquidity and asset prices   10
2.3 Clientele effects   13
2.4 Time-varying transaction costs and liquidity risk   18
2.5 Uncertain trading horizons and liquidity risk   22
2.6 Endogenous trading horizons   23
2.7 Brief aside: Sources of illiquidity   26
2.8 Asset pricing with endogenous illiquidity   31

3 Empirical Evidence   35

3.1 Liquidity measures: Empirical issues   36
3.2 Equity markets   37
3.3 Fixed-income markets   63
3.4 Other financial instruments   73

References   83

1
Introduction*

This survey reviews the literature that studies the relationship between liquidity and asset prices. We review the theoretical literature that predicts how liquidity affects a security's required return and discuss the empirical connection between the two.

Liquidity is a complex concept. Stated simply, liquidity is the ease of trading a security. One source of illiquidity is *exogenous transaction costs* such as brokerage fees, order-processing costs, or transaction taxes. Every time a security is traded, the buyer and/or seller incurs a transaction cost; in addition, the buyer anticipates further costs upon a future sale, and so on, throughout the life of the security.

Another source of illiquidity is *demand pressure* and *inventory risk*. Demand pressure arises because not all agents are present in the market at all times, which means that if an agent needs to sell a security quickly, then the natural buyers may not be immediately available. As a result, the seller may sell to a market maker who buys in anticipation of being able to later lay off the position. The market maker, being exposed to the risk of price changes while he holds the

---

*The authors thank Joel Hasbrouck for helpful comments.

asset in inventory, must be compensated for this risk – a compensation that imposes a cost on the seller.

Also, trading a security may be costly because the traders on the other side may have *private information*. For example, the buyer of a stock may worry that a potential seller has private information that the company is losing money, and the seller may be afraid that the buyer has private information that the company is about to take off. Then, trading with an informed counterparty will end up with a loss. In addition to private information about the *fundamentals* of the security, agents can also have private information about *order flow*. For instance, if a trading desk knows that a hedge fund needs to liquidate a large position and that this liquidation will depress prices, then the trading desk can sell early at relatively high prices and buy back later at lower prices.

Another source of illiquidity is the difficulty of locating a counterparty who is willing to trade a particular security, or a large quantity of a given security. Further, once a counterparty is located, the agents must negotiate the price in a less than perfectly competitive environment since alternative trading partners are not immediately available. This *search friction* is particularly relevant in over-the-counter (OTC) markets in which there is no central marketplace. A searching trader incurs financing costs or opportunity costs as long as his trade is delayed, and, further, he may need to give price concessions in the negotiation with the counterparty that he eventually finds. Alternatively, he may trade quickly with a dealer and bear illiquidity cost. In general, a trader faces a tradeoff between search and quick trading at a discount.

These costs of illiquidity should affect securities prices if investors require compensation for bearing them. In addition, because liquidity varies over time, risk-averse investors may require a compensation for being exposed to liquidity risk. These effects of liquidity on asset prices are important. Investors need to know them in designing their investment strategies. And if liquidity costs and risks affect the required return by investors, they affect corporations' cost of capital and, hence, the allocation of the economy's real resources.

Liquidity has wide ranging effects on financial markets. As our survey shows theoretically and empirically, liquidity can explain the cross-section of assets with different liquidity, after controlling for other assets' characteristics such as risk, and the time series relationship between liquidity and securities returns. Liquidity helps explain why certain hard-to-trade securities are relatively cheap, the pricing of stocks and corporate bonds, the return on hedge funds, and the valuation of closed-end funds. It follows that liquidity can help explain a number of puzzles, such as why equities commanding high required returns (the equity premium puzzle), why liquid risk-free treasuries have low required returns (the risk-free rate puzzle), and why small stocks that are typically illiquid earn high returns (the small firm effect).

The liquidity literature is vast. In this survey we restrict our attention to papers that link liquidity to securities' required return, that is, to the literature on liquidity and asset pricing. Hence, we will not survey the large literature on market microstructure, which studies trading mechanisms and the origins of illiquidity, e.g., in the form of bid–ask spreads or market impact. Surveys of market microstructure include O'Hara (1995), Madhavan (2000), Biais et al. (2002), and Harris (2003). Further, Easley and O'Hara (2003) survey papers on microstructure and the relationship to asset pricing, and Cochrane (2005) surveys recent NBER papers on liquidity and asset pricing. We apologize that we cannot survey every paper on liquidity and asset pricing; the literature is simply too large and too rapidly expanding. Our final apology is that our own papers are probably among the least overlooked; in our defense, these are the papers that we know best, and they ask the questions that originally drew us into this field.

In what follows, the theory of liquidity-based asset pricing is surveyed in Section 2 and the empirical evidence is reviewed in Section 3. The theory section proceeds from basic models with exogenous (expected) holding periods to ones incorporating additional elements of risk and endogenous holding periods. The empirical section reviews the evidence on the liquidity premium for stocks, bonds, and other financial assets.

2
Theory

In this section, we first relate the theory of liquidity and asset pricing to the standard theory of asset pricing in frictionless markets. We then show how liquidity is priced in the most basic model of liquidity, where securities have exogenous trading costs and identical, risk-neutral investors have exogenous trading horizons (Section 2.2). We then extend this basic model to take into account clientele effects (Section 2.3), time-varying trading costs and liquidity risk (Section 2.4), uncertain trading horizons (Section 2.5) and endogenous trading horizons (Section 2.6). We also briefly review the sources of illiquidity and consider models of asset pricing with endogenous illiquidity (Sections 2.7–2.8).

2.1 Liquidity and standard asset pricing theory

To study how liquidity affects asset pricing, it is useful to place it in the context of standard asset pricing theory. Readers may, however, choose to skip directly to Section 2.2, where we start discussing the actual theories of liquidity and asset pricing.

6 Theory

2.1.1 Background: Standard asset pricing

Standard asset pricing[1] is based on the assumption of *frictionless (or, perfectly liquid) markets*, where every security can be traded at no cost all of the time, and *agents take prices as given*. The assumption of frictionless markets is combined with one of the following three concepts: *no arbitrage, agent optimality*, and *equilibrium*.

No arbitrage means that one cannot make money in one state of nature without paying money in at least one other state of nature. In a frictionless market, the assumption of no arbitrage is essentially equivalent to the existence of a stochastic discount factor m_t such that the price process p_t of any security with dividend process d_t satisfies

$$p_t = E_t\left((p_{t+1} + d_{t+1})\frac{m_{t+1}}{m_t}\right). \tag{2.1}$$

Equation (2.1) is the main building block of standard asset pricing theory. It can also be derived from *agent optimality*: if an insatiable investor trades in a frictionless market, his optimal portfolio choice problem only has a solution in the absence of arbitrage – otherwise he will make an arbitrarily large profit and consume an arbitrarily large amount. Further, the first-order condition to the investor's problem has the form (2.1). In particular, if the investor's preferences are represented by an additively separable utility function $E_t \sum_s u_s(c_s)$ for a consumption process c, then $m_t = u'_t(c_t)$ is the marginal utility of consumption.

Finally, in a competitive equilibrium with complete markets and agents $i = 1, \ldots, I$ with separable utility functions u^i, (2.1) is satisfied with $m_t = u'_{t\lambda}(c_t)$, where $u_{t\lambda} = \sum_i \lambda^i u^i_t$ is the utility function of the representative investor and λ_i are the Pareto weights that depend on the agents' endowments.

2.1.2 On the impossibility of frictionless markets

One could argue that, if there were a friction that led to large costs for agents, then there would be an institutional response that would profit by alleviating this friction. According to this view, there cannot be any (important) frictions left in equilibrium.

---
[1] See, for instance, Duffie (1996) or Cochrane (2001).

Alleviating frictions is costly, however, and the institutions which alleviate frictions may be able to earn rents. For instance, setting up a market requires computers, trading systems, clearing operations, risk and operational controls, legal documentation, marketing, information and communication systems, and so on. Hence, if frictions did not affect prices then the institutions that alleviated the frictions would not be compensated for doing so. Therefore, no one would have an incentive to alleviate frictions, and, hence, markets cannot be frictionless.

Grossman and Stiglitz (1980) use a similar argument to rule out informationally efficient markets: market prices cannot fully reveal all relevant information since, if they did, no one would have an incentive to spend resources gathering information in the first place. Hence, investors who collect information must be rewarded through superior investment performance. Therefore, information differences across agents is an equilibrium phenomenon, and this is another source of illiquidity.

There must be an "equilibrium level of disequilibrium," that is, an equilibrium level of illiquidity: the market must be illiquid enough to compensate liquidity providers (or information gatherers), and not so illiquid that it is profitable for new liquidity providers to enter.

2.1.3 Liquidity and asset pricing: The point of departure

If markets are not frictionless, that is, if markets are beset by some form of illiquidity, then the main building blocks of standard asset pricing are shaken. First, the equilibrium aggregation of individual utility functions to a representative investor may not apply. Second, individual investor optimality may not imply that (2.1) holds with $m_t = u'_t(c_t)$ at all times and for all securities. This is because an investor need not be "marginal" on a security if trading frictions make it suboptimal to trade it. Indeed, Luttmer (1996, 1999) shows that trading costs can help explain the empirical disconnect between consumption and asset returns. Hence, illiquidity implies that we cannot easily derive the stochastic discount factor from consumption, much less from aggregate consumption. Then, what determines asset pricing?

8   Theory

Some people might argue that the cornerstone of standard asset pricing is the mere existence of a stochastic discount factor, not necessarily its relation to consumption. Indeed, powerful results – such as the theory of derivative pricing – follow from the simple and almost self-evident premise of no arbitrage. It is, however, important to recognize that the standard no-arbitrage pricing theory relies not only on the absence of arbitrage, but also on the assumption of frictionless markets.

To see why the assumption of frictionless markets is crucial, consider the basic principle of standard asset pricing: securities, portfolios, or trading strategies with the same cash flows must have the same price. This simple principle is based on the insight that, if securities with identical cash flows had different prices, then an investor could buy – with no trading costs – the cheaper security and sell – with no trading costs – the more expensive security, and, hence, realize an immediate arbitrage profit at no risk. Another way to see that standard asset pricing implies that securities with the same cash flows must have the same price is to iterate (2.1) to get

$$p_t = E_t \left(\sum_{s=t+1}^{\infty} d_s \frac{m_s}{m_t} \right), \qquad (2.2)$$

which shows that the price p_t only depends on the pricing kernel and the cash flows d.

With trading costs, however, this principle need not apply. Indeed, with transaction costs, securities with the same cash flows can have different prices without introducing arbitrage opportunities.

Do real-world securities with the same cash flows have the same price? Perhaps surprisingly, the answer is "no," certainly not always. As discussed in Section 3, on-the-run (i.e. newly issued) Treasuries often trade at lower yields than (almost) identical off-the-run Treasuries, and Treasury bills and notes of the same cash flows trade at different prices (Amihud and Mendelson, 1991). Shares that are restricted from trade for two years trade at an average discount of about 30% relative to shares of the same company with identical dividends that can be traded freely (Silber, 1991). Chinese "restricted institutional shares," which can be traded only privately, trade at a discount of about 80% relative to exchange-traded shares in the same company (Chen and Xiong, 2001). Options that cannot be traded over their life trade at large discounts relative to identical tradable options (Brenner et al., 2001). The put–call parity is sometimes violated when it is difficult to sell short, implying that a stock trades at a higher price than a synthetic stock created in the option market (Ofek et al., 2004). Further, in so-called "negative stub value" situations, a security can trade at a lower price than another security, which has strictly lower cash flows (e.g. Lamont and Thaler, 2003).

The existence of securities with identical cash flows and different prices implies that there does not exist a stochastic discount factor m that prices all securities, that is, there does not exist an m such that (2.2) holds for all securities.

Another important difference between standard asset pricing and liquidity asset pricing is that the latter sometimes relaxes the assumption of price-taking behavior. Indeed, if prices are affected by the nature of the trading activity, then agents may take this into account. For instance, if an agent is so large that his trades significantly affect prices, he will take this into account, or if agents trade in a bilateral over-the-counter market, then prices are privately negotiated. Further, the liquidity literature relaxes the assumptions that all investors have the same information and that all investors are present in the market at all times.

2.1.4 Liquidity and asset pricing: Where it will take us (in this survey)

The prices of securities are determined by the general equilibrium of the economy. Hence, the price of a security is some function of the security's cash flow, the cash flows of other securities, the utility functions of all agents, and the agents' endowments. In an economy with frictions, the price depends additionally on the security's liquidity and the liquidity of all other securities.

One strength of a frictionless economy is that a security's cash flows and the pricing kernel are sufficient statistics for the pricing operation described by Equation (2.1). This means that the pricing kernel summarizes all the needed information contained in utility functions, endowments, correlations with other securities, etc.

In some liquidity models, there still exists a pricing kernel m such that (2.1) holds. In this case, illiquidity affects m, but the pricing of securities can still be summarized using a pricing kernel. This is the case if certain agents can trade all securities all of the time without costs. For instance, in the models of demand pressure and inventory risk that follow Grossman and Miller (1988), competitive market makers can trade all securities at no cost (whereas customers can only trade when they arrive in the market). Garleanu et al. (2004) show explicitly how m depends on demand pressure in a multi-asset model. The empirical analysis of Pastor and Stambaugh (2003) is (implicitly) based on an assumption that there exists an m that depends on a measure of aggregate liquidity (but this does not rely on an explicit theory).

In other models of liquidity, however, there is no pricing kernel such that (2.1) applies. For instance, in transaction-cost-based models, securities with the same dividend streams have different prices if they have different transaction costs. Hence, a security's transaction cost not only affects the nature of the equilibrium, it is a fundamental attribute of the security.

When there does not exist a pricing kernel, then the computation of equilibrium asset prices becomes more difficult. Indeed, the general equilibrium prices with illiquidity may depend on the fundamental parameters in a complicated way that does not have a closed-form expression. Nevertheless, we can derive explicit prices under certain special assumptions such as risk neutrality, some structure of trading horizons, partial equilibrium, normally distributed dividends, and so on. While the difficulty of general equilibrium with frictions often forces us to use such special assumptions to get closed-form results, we can still gain important insights into the main principles of how liquidity affects asset prices.

2.2 Basic model of liquidity and asset prices

It is important to understand the effect of liquidity on asset prices in the most basic model. Hence, we consider first a simple model in which securities are illiquid due to exogenous trading costs, and investors are risk neutral and have exogenous trading horizons. This model is a special case of Amihud and Mendelson (1986a).

The basic idea is as follows. A risk-neutral investor who buys a security and expects to pay transaction costs when selling it, will take into account this when valuing the security. She knows that the buyer will also do that, and so on. Consequently, the investor will have to consider, in her valuation, the entire future stream of transaction costs that will be paid on the security. Then, the price discount due to illiquidity is the present value of the expected stream of transaction costs through its lifetime.

Translating this into the required return on the security which is costly to trade, we obtain that the required return is the return that would be required on a similar security which is perfectly liquid, plus the expected trading cost per period, i.e., the product of the probability of trading by the transaction cost.

We consider a simple overlapping generations (OLG) economy in discrete time $t \in \{\ldots, -2, -1, 0, 1, 2, \ldots\}$. There is a perfectly liquid riskless security and agents can borrow and lend at an exogenous risk-free real return of $R^f = 1 + r^f$. Further, there are I illiquid securities indexed by $i = 1, \ldots, I$ with a total of S^i shares of security i. At time t, security i pays a dividend of d_t^i, has an ex-dividend share price of P_t^i, and has an illiquidity cost of $C_t^i = C^i$. The illiquidity cost C^i is modeled simply as the per-share cost of selling security i. Hence, agents can buy at P_t^i but must sell at $P_t^i - C^i$. We assume (for now) that d_t^i are independent and identically distributed (i.i.d.) with mean $\bar{d}^i$.

Agents are risk neutral and have a discount rate of $\frac{1}{R^f}$, and the market prices are determined in a competitive equilibrium. In a competitive equilibrium, agents choose consumption and portfolios so as to maximize their expected utility taking prices as given, and prices are determined such that markets clear. We are looking for a stationary equilibrium, that is, an equilibrium with constant prices P^i.

To fix ideas, suppose first that agents live for two periods and new agents are born every period. If an agent buys a share of security i in the first period of his life, then he must sell the share in the following period, realizing an expected revenue of $\bar{d}^i + P^i - C^i$. The agent will buy an arbitrary large number if shares of the price is lower than the expected discounted revenue $\frac{(\bar{d}^i+P^i-C^i)}{R^f}$, or short an arbitrarily large amount if the price is higher. Hence, we must have

$$P^i = \frac{(\bar{d}^i + P^i - C^i)}{R^f}, \qquad (2.3)$$

implying that

$$P^i = \frac{(\bar{d}^i - C^i)}{r^f}. \qquad (2.4)$$

We see that the price is equal to the present value of all future expected dividends d_i minus the present value of all future transaction costs C^i. This is intuitive. The investor foresees receiving a dividend and paying a transaction cost next period, and he must sell to another investor who foresees the following dividend and transaction cost, and so on.

Alternatively, we can express this result by looking at the effect of liquidity on the required gross return defined as

$$E\left(r^i\right) := E\left(\frac{d^i + P^i}{P^i}\right) - 1 = \frac{\bar{d}^i}{P^i}. \qquad (2.5)$$

We see that the required return is the risk free return increased by the relative transaction cost:

$$E\left(r^i\right) = r^f + \frac{C^i}{P^i}. \qquad (2.6)$$

Equivalently, the liquidity-adjusted expected return is the risk free rate,

$$\frac{\bar{d}^i - C^i}{P^i} = r^f. \qquad (2.7)$$

We can easily generalize this result to an economy in which an agent lives for more than one period. Specifically, suppose that, in any period, an agent must exit the market with some probability μ. This exit event captures the notion of a "liquidity shock" to the agent, for instance, a sudden need for cash. Then, at any time t, the equilibrium price must be the present value of dividends until the random exit time T plus the liquidation value, that is,

$$P^i = E_t \left(\sum_{s=t+1}^{T} \frac{1}{(R^f)^{s-t}} d_t^i + \frac{1}{(R^f)^{T-t}} \left(P^i - C^i \right) \right) \tag{2.8}$$

$$= E_t \left(\sum_{s=t+1}^{\infty} \frac{(1-\mu)^{s-t+1}}{(R^f)^{s-t}} d_t^i \right.$$

$$\left. + \sum_{s=t+1}^{\infty} \frac{\mu(1-\mu)^{s-t+1}}{(R^f)^{s-t}} \left(P^i - C^i \right) \right) \tag{2.9}$$

$$= \frac{1}{r^f + \mu} \left(\bar{d}^i + \mu \left(P^i - C^i \right) \right). \tag{2.10}$$

Rearranging, this implies the following

Proposition 1. When investors are risk neutral with identical trading intensity μ, the equilibrium price of any security i is given by

$$P^i = \frac{\bar{d}^i - \mu C^i}{r^f}. \tag{2.11}$$

or, equivalently, the required return on security i is

$$E\left(r^i\right) = r^f + \mu \frac{C^i}{P^i}. \tag{2.12}$$

Intuitively, (2.11) shows that the price is the expected present value of all future dividends, minus the expected present value of all future transaction costs, taking into account the expected trading frequency μ. The equivalent equation (2.12) shows that the required return is the risk free return plus the per-period percentage transaction cost, that is, the relative transaction cost $\frac{C^i}{P^i}$ weighted by the trading frequency μ.

2.3 Clientele effects

Suppose that investors differ in the likelihood that they need to trade in any period, or in their expected holding period. For example, some investors expect a greater likelihood of a liquidity shock that will force them to liquidate, or a greater likelihood of arrival of a good investment opportunity that will make them want to liquidate their investment

14 *Theory*

and switch to another. Consequently, each investor considers differently the impact of transaction costs on the return that he requires. Since investors require compensation at least for their expected per-period trading costs, a frequently-trading investor requires a higher return than does an infrequently-trading one. A long-term investor who can depreciate the trading cost over a longer (expected) holding period requires lower per-period return than does the short-term investor. Long-term investors can thus outbid the short-term investors on all assets. However, investors have limited resources and cannot buy all assets, and therefore they specialize in investments that are most beneficial for them. While all investors prefer assets with low transaction costs, these assets are most valued by short-term investors who incur transaction costs most frequently. Long-term investors then opt for assets in which they have the greatest advantage – those that are most costly to trade. These illiquid assets are shunned by the frequent traders and are heavily discounted by them. As a result, long-term investors, who bear the costs less frequently, earn rent in holding these assets which *exceeds* their expected transaction costs. Put differently, the liquidity premium on these assets will be *greater* than their expected trading costs. And, in equilibrium, liquid assets are held by frequently-trading investors while the illiquid assets are held by investors with long expected holding period.

This idea is presented by Amihud and Mendelson (1986a), who study the effect of having different types of investors with different expected holding periods. In particular, suppose that an agent of type j, $j = 1, \ldots, J$ receives a liquidity shock with probability μ_j that forces him to sell and leave the market. We number the agent types such that type 1 has the highest risk of a liquidity shock, type 2 has the second highest, and so on, $\mu^1 \geq \mu^2 \geq \cdots \geq \mu^J$. Also, we number the securities such that security 1 is most liquid, security 2 is second most liquid, and so on, $\frac{C^1}{d^1} \leq \frac{C^2}{d^2} \leq \cdots \leq \frac{C^J}{d^J}$.[2]

Agents of type J are the natural buyers of illiquid securities because they have the longest expected holding period and, hence, the smallest

---

[2] Of course, what matters is the transaction cost relative to the fundamental value. In fact, one could use "stock splits" to achieve constant expected dividends for all securities.

2.3. Clientele effects

per-period transaction costs. Hence, without borrowing constraints, the equilibrium is that type-J agents buy all of the illiquid assets and the model reduces to the single-type model of Section 2.2. In this case, transaction costs would matter little as the long-term investors can amortize the trading costs over a long time period. Further, without borrowing constraints, investors could achieve a long holding period by postponing liquidation of assets when facing a cash need and instead financing consumption by borrowing. Hence, borrowing frictions are important for market liquidity to affect prices. See Brunnermeier and Pedersen (2005a) for a discussion of the interaction between market liquidity and borrowing constraints (so-called funding liquidity). In reality, unconstrained borrowing is infeasible. Instead, we make here a convenient (extreme) assumption that agents have limited wealth and cannot borrow. Specifically, agents of type j are born with a wealth of W^j, and there is a mass m^j of agents of type j at any time.

The optimal trading strategy of agent j is to invest all his wealth in securities with the highest liquidity-adjusted return,

$$\max_i \frac{\bar{d}^i - \mu^j C^i}{P^i}, \tag{2.13}$$

and the agent is indifferent among the securities with this maximal liquidity-adjusted return. Note that the liquidity-adjusted return depends both on the security and the agent type.

Amihud and Mendelson (1986a) show that the equilibrium has the following form: The agents with the shortest holding period, i.e., type 1, hold the riskless security and the illiquid securities with the lowest trading cost, i.e. securities $1, \ldots, i^1$ where i^1 is a nonnegative integer. (If $i^1 = 0$ then this means that type 1 agents hold no illiquid securities.) Agents with the next shortest holding period hold a portfolio of securities with the next lowest trading costs, $i^1, \ldots, i^2$ and so on. Hence, agents of type j holds securities $i^{j-1}, \ldots, i^j$ where $0 \leq i^1 \leq i^2 \leq \cdots \leq i^J = I$. The equilibrium cutoff levels, $i^1, \ldots, i^J$ depend on the total wealth of each type of investors. Specifically, type j investors must invest all their wealth in securities $i^{j-1}, \ldots, i^j$, and total demand must equal supply.

Securities with low trading costs are priced such that type 1 agents are indifferent between holding these securities or the risk free asset.

16 Theory

Hence, these securities must offer a liquidity adjusted return equal to the risk free rate,

$$r^f = \frac{\bar{d}^i - \mu^1 C^i}{P^i}, \qquad (2.14)$$

that is,

$$P^i = \frac{\bar{d}^i - \mu^1 C^i}{r^f} \qquad (2.15)$$

for $i = 1, \ldots, i^1$.

With these prices, agents of type 2 earn a return higher than the risk free rate because they have a longer holding period and, hence, pay the trading cost less often. To see this, consider the liquidity-adjusted return of a type-2 agent for a security $i \in \{1, \ldots, i^1\}$:

$$\frac{\bar{d}^i - \mu^2 C^i}{P^i} = \frac{\bar{d}^i - \mu^2 C^i}{\bar{d}^i - \mu^1 C^i} r^f > r^f, \qquad (2.16)$$

since $\mu^2 < \mu^1$. Note that this return is increasing in $\frac{C^i}{\bar{d}^i}$ since the larger is the trading cost, the larger is type-2 agents' comparative advantage. Hence, the largest liquidity-adjusted return is that of security i^1. We denote this return by

$$r^{*2} := \frac{\bar{d}^{i^1} - \mu^2 C^{i^1}}{P^{i^1}}. \qquad (2.17)$$

To make type 2 agents hold securities $i = i^1, \ldots, i^2$, these securities must offer a liquidity-adjusted return of

$$r^{*2} := \frac{\bar{d}^i - \mu^2 C^i}{P^i}, \qquad (2.18)$$

that is,

$$P^i := \frac{\bar{d}^i - \mu^2 C^i}{r^{*2}} \qquad (2.19)$$

for $i^1, \ldots, i^2$.

We can continue this iterative process. In general, a security that is held in equilibrium by type-j investors has a price of

$$P^i := \frac{\bar{d}^i - \mu^j C^i}{r^{*j}} \qquad (2.20)$$

where r^{*j} *is* type-j investors' required liquidity-adjusted return, which is determined by

$$r^{*j} := \frac{\bar{d}^{ij-1} - \mu^j C^{ij-1}}{P^{ij-1}}. \qquad (2.21)$$

Clearly, investors with long horizon earn higher liquidity-adjusted returns (or "rents"), that is, $r^{*1} \leq \cdots \leq r^{*j}$.

Competition among investors implies that the *gross* return on any security is determined by the minimum required return across possible investors:

$$E\left(r^i\right) = \frac{\bar{d}^i}{P^i} = \min_j \left(r^{*j} + \mu^j \frac{C^i}{P^i}\right) \qquad (2.22)$$

Hence, the expected gross return $\frac{\bar{d}^i}{P^i}$ is the minimum of a finite number of increasing linear functions of the relative transaction cost $\frac{C^i}{P^i}$. Since the minimum operator preserves monotonicity and concavity, we have

---

Proposition 2. When investors are risk neutral and clientele j has trading intensity μ^j and limited capital, the equilibrium has the following properties:

(i) Securities with higher transaction costs are allocated to agents with longer (or identical) investment horizons.

(ii) If type j agents are marginal investors for security i, then security i has an expected gross return of

$$E\left(r^i\right) = r^f + \left(r^{*j} - r^f\right) + \mu^j \frac{C^i}{P^i} \qquad (2.23)$$

which is the sum of the risk free rate r^f, investor j's "rent" $\left(r^{*j} - r^f\right)$, and his amortized relative trading cost $\mu^j \frac{C^i}{P^i}$.

(iii) The expected gross return $E\left(r^i\right)$ is an increasing and concave function of the relative transaction cost $\frac{C^i}{P^i}$.

Note that liquid securities are allocated in equilibrium to agents with short investment horizons. Since these agents are the least capable of dealing with illiquidity, they earn lower rents. Therefore, the liquidity premium $(r^{*j} - r^f) + \mu^j \frac{C^i}{P^i}$ for relatively liquid securities arise mostly from the amortized spread $\mu^j \frac{C^i}{P^i}$.

Agents with long investment horizons, however, can earn rents because patient capital is in short supply. Hence, according to this clientele theory, the liquidity premium $(r^{*j} - r^f) + \mu^j \frac{C^i}{P^i}$ for relatively illiquid securities arise largely from the rents $(r^{*j} - r^f)$ and less from the amortized spread because the relevant μ^j is small.[3]

2.4 Time-varying transaction costs and liquidity risk

Liquidity varies over time.[4] This means that investors are uncertain what transactions cost they will incur in the future when they need to sell an asset. Further, since liquidity affects the level of prices, liquidity fluctuations can affect the asset price volatility itself. For both of these reasons, liquidity fluctuations constitute a new type of risk that augments the fundamental cash-flow risk. This section presents a model of the effect of a security's liquidity risk on its expected return, thus extending the standard Sharpe–Lintner–Mossin effect of risk on expected return. The exposition follows Acharya and Pedersen (2005) dynamic OLG model of the effect of variations in liquidity on asset prices under risk aversion. The model gives rise to a liquidity-adjusted capital asset pricing model that shows how liquidity risk is captured by three liquidity betas, and how shocks to liquidity affect current prices and future expected returns. A static asset pricing model with uncertain trading costs is presented by Jacoby et al. (2000).

To make the model tractable, we assume that agents live for only one period (that is, $\mu = 1$). Generation t consists of N agents, indexed by n, who live for two periods, t and $t + 1$. Agent n of generation t has an endowment at time t and no other sources of income, trades in periods t and $t + 1$, and derives utility from consumption at time $t + 1$. He has constant absolute risk aversion A^n so that his preferences are

---

[3] See Kane (1994) for an alternative proof of the clientele effect. In a static mode without clientele effects, Jacoby et al. (2000) show that short-lived securities' required return can be convex in trading costs.
[4] Brunnermeier and Pedersen (2005a) offer a model that explains the variations over time in liquidity, linking it to variations in the funding conditions of market makers.

2.4. Time-varying transaction costs and liquidity risk

represented by the expected utility function $-E_t \exp(-A^n x_{t+1})$, where x_{t+1} is his consumption at time $t+1$.

Uncertainty about the illiquidity cost is what generates the liquidity risk in this model. Specifically, we assume that d_t^i and C_t^i are autoregressive processes of order one, that is:

$$d_t = \bar{d} + \rho^D \left(d_{t-1} - \bar{d}\right) + \varepsilon_t \tag{2.24}$$

and

$$C_t = \bar{C} + \rho^C \left(C_{t-1} - \bar{C}\right) + \eta_t, \tag{2.25}$$

where $\bar{d}, \bar{C} \in \Re_+^I$ are positive real vectors, $\rho^D, \rho^C \in [0,1]$, and (ϵ_t, η_t) is an independent identically distributed normal process.

We are interested in how an asset's expected gross return,

$$r_t^i = \frac{d_t^i + P_t^i}{P_{t-1}^i} - 1, \tag{2.26}$$

depends on its relative illiquidity cost,

$$c_t^i = \frac{C_t^i}{P_{t-1}^i}, \tag{2.27}$$

on the market return,

$$r_t^M = \frac{\sum_i S^i \left(d_t^i + P_t^i\right)}{\sum_i S^i P_{t-1}^i} - 1, \tag{2.28}$$

and on the relative market illiquidity,

$$c_t^M = \frac{\sum_i S^i C_t^i}{\sum_i S^i P_{t-1}^i}. \tag{2.29}$$

To determine the equilibrium prices, consider first an economy with the same agents in which asset i has a dividend of $D_t^i - C_t^i$ and no illiquidity cost. In this imagined economy, standard results imply that the CAPM holds (Lintner, 1965; Markowitz, 1952; Mossin, 1966; Sharpe,

1964). We claim that the equilibrium prices in the original economy with frictions are the same as those of the imagined economy. This follows from two facts: (i) the net return on a long position is the same in both economies; and, (ii) all investors in the imagined economy hold a long position in the market portfolio, and a (long or short) position in the risk-free asset. Hence, an investor's equilibrium return in the frictionless economy is feasible in the original economy, and is also optimal, since positive transactions costs imply that a short position has a worse payoff than minus the payoff of a long position.

These arguments show that the CAPM in the imagined frictionless economy translates into a CAPM in net returns for the original economy with illiquidity costs. Rewriting the one-beta CAPM in net returns in terms of gross returns, we get a liquidity-adjusted CAPM for gross returns. To capture this, Acharya and Pedersen (2005) introduce three liquidity betas β^{L1}, β^{L2}, and β^{L3}, which complement the standard market beta β:

Proposition 3 (Liquidity-Adjusted CAPM). When investors are risk averse and liquidity and dividends are risky as specified above, the conditional expected net return of security i in the unique linear equilibrium is

$$E_t\left(r_{t+1}^i - c_{t+1}^i\right) = r^f + \lambda_t \frac{\mathrm{cov}_t\left(r_{t+1}^i - c_{t+1}^i, r_{t+1}^M - c_{t+1}^M\right)}{\mathrm{var}_t\left(r_{t+1}^M - c_{t+1}^M\right)}, \quad (2.30)$$

where $\lambda_t = E_t\left(r_{t+1}^M - c_{t+1}^M - r^f\right)$ is the risk premium. Equivalently, the conditional expected gross return is:

$$E_t\left(r_{t+1}^i\right) = r^f + E_t\left(c_{t+1}^i\right) + \lambda_t\left(\beta_t + \beta_t^{L1} - \beta_t^{L2} - \beta_t^{L3}\right), \quad (2.31)$$

where

$$\beta_t = \frac{\mathrm{cov}_t\left(r_{t+1}^i, r_{t+1}^M\right)}{\mathrm{var}_t\left(r_{t+1}^M - c_{t+1}^M\right)}, \quad (2.32)$$

$$\beta_t^{L1} = \frac{\mathrm{cov}_t\left(c_{t+1}^i, c_{t+1}^M\right)}{\mathrm{var}_t\left(r_{t+1}^M - c_{t+1}^M\right)}, \quad (2.33)$$

$$\beta_t^{L2} = \frac{\mathrm{cov}_t\left(r_{t+1}^i, c_{t+1}^M\right)}{\mathrm{var}_t\left(r_{t+1}^M - c_{t+1}^M\right)}, \quad (2.34)$$

and

$$\beta_t^{L3} = \frac{\text{cov}_t\left(c_{t+1}^i, r_{t+1}^M\right)}{\text{var}_t\left(r_{t+1}^M - c_{t+1}^M\right)}. \tag{2.35}$$

Equation (2.31) is simple and natural. It states that the required excess return is the expected relative illiquidity cost, $E_t\left(c_{t+1}^i\right)$ as in the basic model above, plus four betas (or covariances) times the risk premium. These four betas depend on the asset's payoff and liquidity risks. As in the standard CAPM, the required return on an asset increases linearly with the market beta, that is, the covariance between the asset's return and the market return. This model yields three additional effects which could be regarded as three forms of liquidity risks.

The first liquidity beta β^{L1} is positive for most securities due to commonality in liquidity.[5] The model implies that expected return increases with the covariance between the asset's illiquidity and the market illiquidity, because investors want to be compensated for holding a security that becomes illiquid when the market in general becomes illiquid.

The second liquidity beta β^{L2}, which measures the exposure of asset i to marketwide illiquidity, is usually negative[6] in part because a rise in market illiquidity reduces asset values. This beta affects required returns negatively because investors are willing to accept a lower return on an asset with a high return in times of market illiquidity. Consequently, the more negative is the exposure of the asset to marker illiquidity, the greater is the required return.

The third liquidity beta β^{L3} is also negative for most stocks.[7] This liquidity beta has a negative sign in the pricing model, meaning that the required return is higher if the sensitivity of the security's illiquidity to market condition is more negative. The negative effect stems from the willingness of investors to accept a lower expected return on a security that is liquid in a down market. When the market declines, investors are poor and the ability to sell easily is especially valuable. Hence, an

---

[5] See evidence in Hasbrouck and Seppi (2001), Huberman and Halka (2001), Chordia et al. (2002).
[6] See evidence in Amihud (2002).
[7] See evidence in Acharya and Pedersen (2005) and Chordia et al. (2005).

investor is willing to accept a discounted return on stocks with low illiquidity costs in states of poor market return.

Empirically, liquidity is persistent over time,[8] meaning that if a market is illiquid today, then it is more likely to not fully recover next month. Mathematically, this means that $\rho^C > 0$.

Acharya and Pedersen (2005) show that persistence of liquidity implies that liquidity predicts future returns (Equation (2.36) below) and co-moves with contemporaneous returns (Equation (2.37) below). Intuitively, as stated in Amihud (2002), a high illiquidity today predicts a high expected illiquidity next period, implying a high required return, which is achieved by lowering current prices. This result relies on the realistic assumption that cash flow shocks and shocks to the trading costs are not too highly correlated.

Proposition 4. Assuming that liquidity is persistent and certain technical conditions are satisfied for a portfolio q, then an increase in illiquidity implies that the required return increases:

$$\frac{\partial}{\partial C_t^q} E_t \left(r_{t+1}^q - r^f \right) > 0 \tag{2.36}$$

and contemporaneous returns are low

$$\text{cov}_{t-1} \left(c_t^q, r_t^q \right) < 0. \tag{2.37}$$

2.5 Uncertain trading horizons and liquidity risk

In the previous section, we considered the risk that it suddenly becomes very costly to liquidate a portfolio. Another way of considering liquidity risk is to focus on the trading horizon, while keeping the trading costs constant.

The net-of-transaction-cost rate of return (per unit of time) of an asset is increasing with the holding period since the transaction cost is depreciated over a longer period and thus its per-period effect is smaller. If the holding period becomes stochastic due to liquidity shocks, the net

---

[8] See evidence in Amihud (2002).

return becomes random as well even if both the gross return and the transaction costs are deterministic. In the basic model of Section 2.2, this risk is ignored since agents are assumed risk neutral. If agents are risk averse, then this liquidity-induced risk will be priced. Huang (2003) analyzes this problem, assuming two console bonds that are identical except that one is liquid and the other is illiquid, i.e., it incurs proportional transaction costs. Investors are risk averse (with CARA utility function) and have a constant income stream. Each investor is hit by a negative "liquidity shock" with a Poisson arrival rate and, when this happens, the investor must liquidate his securities and exit. Importantly, there is a constraint on short selling and on borrowing against future income. Thus, the transaction costs that the investor incurs upon liquidation negatively affect his immediate consumption and he cannot alleviate this effect by borrowing. This effect would be particularly costly (in terms of utility of consumption) if the investor has just recently acquired the illiquid asset, in which case the return that has accumulated on it is small relative to the liquidation costs. Huang shows that in equilibrium, the illiquid security whose net return becomes stochastic will have a premium over the liquid security which exceeds the magnitude of expected transaction costs, reflecting the liquidity-induced risk premium. This can help explain why the return premium on illiquid stocks, estimated in empirical studies, is so large relative to expected per-period transaction costs.

Vayanos (2004) considers a model in which investors' risk of needing to liquidate is time varying and shows that the liquidity premium – that is, the return compensation for illiquidity – is also time varying. Indeed, when investors have a high likelihood of needing to sell, the liquidity premium is high. Further, Vayanos (2004) links the risk of needing to liquidate to the market volatility.

2.6 Endogenous trading horizons

The models considered so far have assumed that the trading horizon was exogenous, that is, μ was exogenous. In many cases, however, trading horizons are the outcome of optimal investor behavior, and investors can trade off cost and benefits of delaying trades. To capture this effect, Constantinides (1986) studies a continuous-time model in which an investor with constant relative risk aversion holds a risk free and a risky security, the latter having proportional exogenous trading cost.[9] Absent trading costs, theory suggests that the investor will hold a fixed ratio of the assets and trade continuously to balance his portfolio in response to the risky asset's price changes. With trading costs, the investor faces a tradeoff: frequent portfolio rebalancing when the risky/riskless assets ratio deviates from its optimal value entails high trading costs, while refraining from rebalancing renders the portfolio suboptimal and imposes a utility cost. The solution is setting a boundary around (above and below) the optimal asset ratio within which there is no trading, and when the ratio is outside of the boundary, the investor transacts to the nearest boundary.[10] The width of the no-trade region increases in the risky security's trading costs, and thus higher trading costs lead to less trading, less demand for the risky asset, and a higher utility loss for the investor. The liquidity premium on the risky asset with trading costs is then defined as the decrease in its expected return that would leave the investor indifferent between this asset and an identical asset with no trading costs. Using calibrated parameter values, Constantinides finds that the liquidity premium in terms of per-annum return is an order of magnitude smaller than the trading cost. This is because investors in his model can largely alleviate the cost by reduced trading and because the utility costs of not trading are small.

Vayanos (1998) constructs a general equilibrium model with endogenous trading horizons. Overlapping generations of investors trade and consume continuously over their deterministic lifespan and have access to a perfectly liquid riskless asset and to a general number of risky assets that are costly to trade. In equilibrium, investors buy the risky

---

[9] See also Liu (2004a) who determine the optimal trading strategy for an investor with constant absolute risk aversion and many independent securities with both fixed and proportional costs.

[10] Constantinides (1986) assumes that the investor continuously consumes a constant proportion of riskless wealth. Davis and Norman (1990) prove formally that the optimal investment indeed is bang-bang as assumed by Constantinides (1986) and derive the optimal consumption, which is, however, not a constant proportional of riskless wealth. While the investor behavior considered by Constantinides (1986) is therefore not fully optimal, the order of magnitude of Constantinides's calibration results has not been questioned.

assets when born, and slowly sell them as they become older and more risk averse. A calibration of the model finds that the effects of transaction costs are small because life-cycle is the only trading motive (similar to Constantinides (1986)). Further, Vayanos shows that a general equilibrium model with endogenous horizons can lead to surprising results. For instance, in certain special cases, transaction costs can actually raise an asset's price. This can happen because, while trading costs make investors buy fewer shares, they induce them to hold the shares for longer periods, which can raise the total asset demand.

Some of the observed evidence in the market is consistent with these models' predictions. We observe that in the last decade there has been a significant decline in trading costs in U.S. stock markets, partly due to reducing the minimum tick from $\$\frac{1}{8}$ to $\$\frac{1}{16}$ and then to a penny. At the same time, stock turnover in the New York Stock Exchange has risen from 54% in 1994 to 99% in 2004.[11] This relationship is predicted, e.g., by Constantinides's model, where the width of the no-trade region increases in trading costs. However, the liquidity premium predicted by these models is low relative to the empirical results documented in Section 3, reflecting the models' assumptions that the only reason for trading is portfolio rebalancing where the parameters of the risky asset's process are constant.[12] Further, due to this minor need for trade, the annual turnover predicted, e.g., by Vayanos is around 3%, which is quite low relative to observed turnover.

In the real world, many investors have larger needs to trade in spite of the significant trading costs. A simple reduced-form way of capturing a large trading need is to use the models of Sections 2.2–2.5 with a trading intensity calibrated to match the observed volume. Further, the following studies introduce additional motives for trade in models with endogenous trading horizon and, consequently, obtain that the effect of trading costs on the liquidity premium is greater. Lo et al. (2004) consider an equilibrium with two completely "opposite" agents who have perfectly negatively correlated endowment risk. The agents face fixed per-trade trading costs so they refrain from trading when the security

---

[11] Source: NYSE Fact Book 2004.
[12] Novy-Marx (2005) describes how liquidity can appear to be priced (as in the empirical literature) even when its not, because liquidity can proxy for unobserved risk factors.

position is within certain boundaries and, when the position reaches a boundary, they trade to the optimal position somewhere in the middle of the no-trade region (as oppose to trading to nearest boundary as is as the case with proportional trading costs). Lo et al. (2004) find that the liquidity premium can be large when the investors have high-frequency trading needs. Also, the partial equilibrium approach of Constantinides (1986) has been extended by Jang et al. (2005) who introduce a time-varying investment opportunity set, and Lynch and Tan (2004) who consider return predictability, wealth shocks, and state-dependent transaction costs.[13] These motivations for trading in excess of Constantinides (1986) portfolio rebalancing motive increase the resulting trading frequency and the impact of transaction costs on price. These authors show through numerical calibration that the liquidity premium can be large for certain parameters that they find realistic.

Vayanos and Vila (1999) study an OLG model with a risky asset with proportional trading costs and a liquid riskless asset in fixed supply, thus endogenizing the riskless interest rate. If the risky asset has a higher trading cost then the risk-free asset becomes a more attractive alternative. Therefore, the equilibrium price of the risk-free asset is increasing (i.e., the risk-free interest rate is decreasing) in the trading cost of the risky asset. Heaton and Lucas (1996) solve an equilibrium model of incomplete risk sharing numerically and find that trading costs increase the equity premium and lower the riskfree rate. Heaton and Lucas (1996) find sizeable effects only if trading costs are large or the quantity of traded assets is small.

2.7 Brief aside: Sources of illiquidity

As discussed in the introduction, illiquidity can arise from exogenous trading costs, private information, inventory risk for market makers, and search problems. While the illiquidity related to exogenous costs and search are straightforward, we briefly review how information and inventory problems can also lead to illiquidity. In Section 2.8 we discuss how these sources of illiquidity affect security prices.

---

[13] See also Balduzzi and Lynch (1999).

2.7.1 Illiquidity deriving from private information

Certain investors or corporate insiders can have superior information (or information processing ability) about the fundamental value of a security. This creates an adverse selection problem: informed traders with bad news are likely to sell, and informed traders with good news have an incentive to buy (Akerlof, 1970).

Grossman and Stiglitz (1980) show that information asymmetries are fundamental to market equilibrium for, if all information were contained in prices, no one has an incentive to gather information in the first place. Hence, they consider a noisy rational expectations equilibrium (REE) in which investors are competitive price takers who learn from prices. In equilibrium, some investors refrain from collecting information while others incur cost in gathering information and get compensated in the form of superior expected investment performance such that the two groups of investors have the same overall expected utility. The literature on how information is revealed through prices in REE also includes Grossman (1976), Hellwig (1980), Admati (1985), and others.

Investors with private information have an incentive to strategically take into account the price effect of their trades, and market makers strategically protect themselves against informed traders. Bagehot (1971) proposes that the market maker gains from trading with uninformed liquidity traders and loses money to informed traders. This gives rise to the bid-ask spread, which is necessary to compensate the market maker for his losses to the informed traders. Copeland and Galai (1983) model the quoting decision of a profit-maximizing market maker, with profit defined as the difference between the gain from liquidity traders and the loss to informed traders. Copeland and Galai view the quoted bid and ask prices as strike prices on two free options with a very short expiration period written by the market maker to the informed trader. The ask and bid prices are, respectively, the strike (exercise) prices of the call and of the put, straddling the current security's price. The model's implication is that increased uncertainty (volatility) widens the spread, which concurs with the empirical evidence.

A standard way of modeling the market maker's strategy when trading with informed investors is to assume that the market maker is competitive and risk neutral with a discount rate equal to the risk-free rate, which is normalized to zero. Such a competitive market maker sets the price p_t at time t according to

$$p_t = E(v|\Im_t, OF_t), \qquad (2.38)$$

where v is the fundamental value, $\Im_t$ is the public information, and OF_t is the order flow at time t. Hence, the market maker sets a price equal to his best estimate of the asset's fundamental value, given what he learns from the order flow. With this price-setting principle, execution prices follow a martingale.

This general modeling approach is applied in the context of various market structures. Glosten and Milgrom (1985) consider a market structure in which competitive market makers must quote binding bid and ask prices and investors arrive sequentially and can decide whether to buy one share at the ask, sell one share at the bid, or refrain from trading. In this case, the bid is the expected value of the fundamental given that the next trade is a sell order, and similarly for the ask, leading to the following "regret free" prices:

$$\text{bid}_t = E(v|\Im_t, \text{ sell}), \qquad (2.39)$$

and

$$\text{ask}_t = E(v|\Im_t, \text{ buy}). \qquad (2.40)$$

The quoted bid price reflects the risk that a seller is informed of bad news, and the ask reflects the risk that a buyer is informed of good news. If the market maker were sure that the counterparty is informed, she would not trade at all since as long as the informed trader wishes to sell, the price is too high. What makes the market maker willing to trade is the possibility that the counterparty is uninformed, and it may gain by selling to him at a "high"-ask-price or buying from him at a "low"-bid-price. Thus, the market maker gains from trading with uninformed traders and looses to informed ones. Since in a competitive market the market maker ends up with zero profit, the gains of the informed traders are at the expense of the uninformed trade. Clearly, the model implies a bid–ask spread (bid $<$ ask) which is greater if the probability of trading with informed traders is larger.

2.7. Brief aside: Sources of illiquidity

Kyle (1985) considers a market where an informed and an uninformed "noise" trader each submit a market order for an asset, and the market maker sets the price depending on the aggregate order flow such that he ends up with zero gain (as is the case in a competitive market). A large demand will make the market maker raise the price since it may reflect demand by an informed investor who knows that the asset value is high. The noise trader submits an exogenous normally distributed order u, while the informed trader optimally decides on his order x given his signal about the value v, where x is constrained by the informed trader's knowledge that a large order will reveal his information to the market maker and will cause the price to be set closer to v, leaving him with a smaller per-unit gain.[14] Kyle shows that there exists a linear equilibrium in which the market maker sets the price as

$$p_t = E\left(v | \Im_t, u_t + x_t\right) = p_{t-1} + \lambda_t \left(u_t + x_t\right), \qquad (2.41)$$

where λ describes the price change per unit of net order flow, that is, the market impact, which is a measure of illiquidity. Kyle shows that λ increases in the variance about v, i.e., in the extent of asymmetry in information, and it declines in the variance of u, the uninformed investors' order flow.[15] Thus, both the bid–ask spread and the market impact are measures of market illiquidity that can result from information asymmetry. Mendelson and Tunca (2004) extend the Kyle (1985) model to the case of endogenous liquidity trading. Like Kyle (1985) and the other papers briefly reviewed in this subsection, they do not address how information asymmetry affects required return.

Whereas the above-mentioned papers deal with the effects of private information about fundamental news, there is also a more recent literature that recognizes the importance of private information about order flow; for example, a trader might be using his knowledge about someone else moving a large block of shares. This literature includes Madrigal

---

[14] In this model, the informed trader is a monopolist on the information on v and he thus acts as a monopolist who considers the consequences of his action on price.

[15] Admati and Pfleiderer (1988) further show how private information leads to endogenous concentration of trade since all traders prefer to trade at the time of highest liquidity, Kyle (1989) considers the case of imperfect competition between market makers, and Easley and O'Hara (1987) study the information content of trade side and its consequent effect on prices.

(1996) who considers non-fundamental speculation, Attari et al. (2005) and Brunnermeier and Pedersen (2005b) who study predatory trading (trading the exploits or induces other traders need to liquidate a position),[16] Vayanos (2001) and Cao et al. (2003) who consider strategic trading due to risk sharing, and Gallmeyer et al. (2004) who study uncertainty about the preferences of potential counterparties.

2.7.2 Illiquidity deriving from inventory risk

A fundamental source of illiquidity is the fragmentation of investors and markets due to the fact that not all investors are present in the same market all of the time. For instance, a seller may arrive to the market at a time when a natural buyer is not present. This gap between the seller and buyer is bridged by market makers who provide immediacy through their continuous presence in the market and thus enable continuous trading by any trader who so wishes. In particular, the market maker can buy from the seller and later resell to the buyer. However, the market maker faces a risk of fundamental price changes in the meantime and must be compensated for this risk. This has been pointed out by Stoll (1978a). Garman (1976) introduces a model with a monopolist market maker whose quoted prices affect the intensity of arrival of buyers and sellers. If quoted prices are constant, the market maker will be surely ruined. Amihud and Mendelson (1980) and Ho and Stoll (1981) resolve this problem by having the quoted bid–ask prices depend on the market maker's inventory of the traded security. Amihud and Mendelson assume a market maker who constrains his inventory position (due to capital constraint and risk) and manages inventory to avoid the constraints, and Ho and Stoll assume a risk-averse market maker who manages inventory to reduce his risk exposure. Demand-pressure models with competitive market makers are considered by Ho and Stoll (1983) and Grossman and Miller (1988). Brunnermeier and Pedersen (2005a) relate variations in liquidity over time and cross-sectionally to market makers' capital constraints.

---

[16] See also Pritsker (2003)

2.8 Asset pricing with endogenous illiquidity

In Section 2.7 we described how illiquidity can arise endogenously due to various fundamental frictions. We are interested in determining how these frictions ultimately affect asset prices. One approach is to take the endogenously derived liquidity costs and "plug them into" the asset pricing models with exogenous trading costs (Sections 2.2–2.6). As we show below, we can sometimes get additional insights by considering asset pricing directly in a model of endogenous illiquidity.

2.8.1 Private information and the required return

The effect of information asymmetry on the required return is studied in dynamic REE models by Wang (1993, 1994) and in a strategic model by Garleanu and Pedersen (2004). Wang (1993) considers a dynamic infinite-horizon model in which all investors observe a dividend process and the corresponding stock price, but only a fraction of the investors observe the dividend process's stochastic growth rate Π. The price does not fully reveal Π since the supply of shares is random. Wang shows that if there is a larger fraction of less-informed investors who do not observe Π, then the required return is higher. One reason for this is that when dividends increase, less-informed investors increase their expectations of dividend growth, thus pushing prices up. This process raises the correlation of prices and dividends, thus raising total return volatility, which reduces consumption smoothing and risk sharing and increases the average risk premium.[17]

Garleanu and Pedersen (2004) consider a model in which a finite number of agents trade repeatedly by submitting market or limit orders. Each period, one agent may receive a signal about the next dividend, and potentially a "liquidity shock." Garleanu and Pedersen show that, if agents are *symmetric* ex ante, then future bid–ask spreads due to private information are not a direct trading cost. That is, their present value does not directly reduce the price – unlike the case of exogenous trading costs. This result obtains because, in expectation, the future

---
[17] Recent static models of asymmetric information and asset prices include Easley and O'Hara (2004) and O'Hara (2003).

losses an agent will incur when trading due to liquidity reasons are balanced by the gains he will make when trading based on information. If the agents differ ex ante, though, in that some agents are more likely to make liquidity trades than others, then the marginal investor does not break even on average and her expected net trading losses augment the required return. Importantly, the adverse-selection problems lead to an indirect cost associated with allocation inefficiencies caused by trading-decision distortions. This indirect allocation cost (further) increases the required return.

2.8.2 Illiquidity due to inventory-risk and demand pressure

From the investor's viewpoint, illiquidity due to demand pressure and inventory-related costs can be treated as exogenous illiquidity cost, whose effect on asset prices are as derived in Sections 2.2–2.6. The smaller the inventory position that the market maker is willing to assume due to reasons such as the risk of his position or limits on his capital (Amihud and Mendelson, 1980; Brunnermeier and Pedersen, 2005a), or the greater the price volatility of the security traded (Ho and Stoll, 1981), the greater is the bid–ask spread that the market maker sets. In addition, variations in demand pressure that cause variations in the market maker inventory change the prices at which he is willing to trade. These are short-term, transitory effects of inventory on prices, but the permanent effect on prices and expected return flows through the effect on trading costs. For example, in market systems with better capacity to absorb inventory shocks, the models would predict smaller illiquidity costs and consequently there would be smaller price discount due to illiquidity.

2.8.3 Search, bargaining, and limits on trading

Liquidity problems often play a role in "over the counter" (OTC) markets, that is, when there is no centralized market and investors trade bilaterally, for instance over the phone. In such markets, illiquidity arises because of search and bargaining problems. For instance, when a trader needs to sell her position, she must search for a counterparty willing to buy, and, once a potential counterparty is located, the trader

2.8. Asset pricing with endogenous illiquidity

must negotiate the price – a negotiation that reflects each trader's outside option to find other counterparties. Further, due to the bilateral trading in OTC markets, intermediaries can have market power, allowing them to earn fees, which translate into trading costs for investors. Duffie et al. (2003, 2005) model such search and bargaining features and study how these sources of illiquidity affect asset prices. They find that, under certain conditions, search frictions increase the liquidity premium (i.e., lower prices) and increase bid–ask spreads. Further, higher bargaining power to buyers leads to lower prices. Also, Duffie et al. (2003) link volatility to liquidity and thus to prices.

Weill (2002) and Vayanos and Wang (2002) extend the model of Duffie, Garleanu and Pedersen to the case of multiple illiquid securities and show, among other things, that search frictions lead to cross-sectional differences in the liquidity premium. In particular, securities with larger float (or supply) of securities are predicted to have less severe search problems and correspondingly lower liquidity premia. Lagos (2005) shows that search frictions can help explain the risk-free rate and equity-premium puzzles.

Vayanos and Wang (2002) further show how search externalities can lead to concentration of trade in one security among several substitutes. Duffie et al. (2002) consider a model in which shortsellers must search for lendable securities, and must negotiate the lending fee with the lender, thus capturing the real-world OTC institution for short-selling. They show how the lending fee initially increases the value of the security. Vayanos and Weill (2005) develop a multi-asset model in which both the spot markets (for buying and selling securities) and the securities lending markets (for borrowing shares to shortsell) are OTC search markets. In equilibrium, one security is "special": it is liquid, has a high price, and has a large lending fee. Boudoukh and Whitelaw (1993) show that it can be in the issuer's interest to maintain segmented markets in which one security is special.

Hopenhayn and Werner (1996) consider a matching model in which certain assets have payoffs that are "non-verifiable" to uninformed agents. When uninformed agents are matched, they do not trade assets with non-verifiable payoffs and, therefore, these assets become less liquid and have a higher expected return.

Longstaff (1995) considers the liquidity premium in a partial equilibrium model with limited access to counterparties using a different approach. A hypothetical investor can perfectly predict the future price movements of a security over a certain time period but cannot trade the security during this period. If the investor could time the sale of the asset optimally, it would be worth more than if he has to hold it until the end of the period. The difference – the value of the foregone option to sell the asset optimally – is an upper bound on the value of liquidity. The value of liquidity can also be likened then to the payoff from an option on the maximum value of a security whose exercise (strike) price is the value of the security when the liquidity restriction expires. This option is also in the money, meaning that there is a positive liquidity discount. Longstaff then obtains that the maximum value of this option when the restriction period is 2 years and volatility is 30% is 38.6% of the asset value – quite close to the discount observed for restricted stock (see Section 3.2.4 below). It is of course questionable whether investors can perfectly time their trades, therefore the price discount in this model is the upper bound on the cost of illiquidity. But the method can be used for *any* strategy that investors wish to apply based on observables, and then the cost of illiquidity is the opportunity cost of foregoing this strategy.

Longstaff (2001) considers a continuous-time model in which an investor must limit his trading intensity, thus capturing the idea that investors cannot unwind a position immediately. Consequently, the investor must avoid shorting or taking a leveraged positions, i.e., his investment in the risky asset is limited (the model is in partial equilibrium). Longstaff derives the optimal portfolio choice under this constraint, and shows numerically that the implied liquidity premium can be substantial. This trading friction is also used by Brunnermeier and Pedersen (2005b) who study the asset pricing effects of illiquidity deriving from predatory trading. They show that a trader who needs to sell a large position is exploited by other traders, and this endogenous illiquidity raises the required return ex-ante.

3

Empirical Evidence

Conceptually, the first research question to be addressed by empirical studies of liquidity and asset pricing is regarding the *existence* of a liquidity effect. As discussed in Section 2.1.3, the null hypothesis of standard asset pricing theory is that assets with the same cash flow d should have the same price. To test the existence of a liquidity effect, the researcher identifies two assets 1 and 2 with cash flows d^1 and d^2 and different measures of liquidity L^1 and L^2 and examines the asset prices, P^1 and P^2, at the same point in time. If asset 1 is more liquid, i.e., $L^1 > L^2$, but the assets have the same cash flow, $d^1 = d^2$, standard asset pricing theory implies the null hypothesis $P^1 = P^2$, whereas liquidity-based asset pricing implies the alternative hypothesis $P^1 > P^2$. In some cases, asset 1 is a synthetic security designed to replicate the cash flow pattern d^2 of asset 2, so the price P^1 is only an estimate of the price of the synthetic security, typically based on theoretical considerations. Surely, the pricing differences between assets may also be estimated by looking at differences in their expected returns or yields, assuming the same cash flows or controlling for differences in other determinants of expected returns. In some cases, the researcher examines a family of assets with different cash flows and different levels of liquidity. Then, the analysis includes control variables that account for the differences that can be explained by the different cash flows, and then tests whether the price differential which is unexplained by the control variables is significantly related to differences in liquidity.

As we discuss below, the empirical evidence supports the existence of a liquidity effect, leading to a rejection of the null hypothesis. This leads to the second research question: What is the magnitude and functional form of the liquidity effect? This can be studied either cross-sectionally, comparing prices for a family of assets with different levels of liquidity (using adequate controls), or in a time-series study, where the liquidity of a given security changes over time and the researcher studies the price change associated with the liquidity change.

The empirical work on liquidity and asset pricing often combines the two research questions, focusing on the effects of liquidity on a family of financial instruments which vary in their liquidity. Accordingly, we classify the empirical literature based on the financial instruments used to test and estimate the liquidity effect. We start by examining the relationship between liquidity and asset prices for stocks, where the liquidity effect has been studied extensively. Within this class, we distinguish between cross-section tests and studies of the effect of changes in liquidity over time, examine separately studies that focus on the effects of liquidity risk (rather than the level of liquidity) on asset prices, and conclude with the effects of trading restrictions on stock prices. We then review empirical work that studies the effect of liquidity on bond yields, distinguishing between U.S. Treasury securities and corporate bonds, which pose the additional challenge of disentangling the effects of liquidity and default risk. We then review the literature on liquidity and asset prices for other financial instruments – options, index-linked bonds, American Depository Receipts (ADRs), hedge funds and closed-end funds.

We consider first the challenges of choosing a liquidity measure L.

3.1 Liquidity measures: Empirical issues

As pointed out in Section 2, liquidity has a many facets. A major problem in estimating the effect of liquidity on asset prices or returns is how to measure liquidity since there is hardly a single measure that captures all of its aspects. In addition, measures used in empirical studies are constrained by data availability. High-frequency data that enable the estimation of liquidity from the actual sequence of trades and quotes became available in the U.S. only recently and are thus available only for a relatively short period of time. Further, studies of the effect of liquidity on expected stock returns use ex-post or realized returns, whose variance around the expected return is high. Consequently, researchers need a large amount of data – long time series – to increase the power of their tests. Given the short duration of high-frequency data, this poses a problem. Researchers need then to find substitute measures of liquidity using low-frequency data, such as daily return data and perhaps trading volume. In stock markets outside the U.S., high frequency data are hardly available, and the researcher then needs to estimate liquidity from daily return data, and, if available, from volume data as well. The empirical studies we survey thus employ various measures of liquidity, obtained from both high frequency and daily data. Neither is a perfect measure of liquidity, but most of these measures are highly positively correlated.

These problems in the measurement of liquidity reduce the power of tests of the effect of liquidity on securities pricing. Any liquidity measure used clearly measures liquidity with an error, because (i) a single measure cannot capture all the different dimensions of liquidity, (ii) the empirically-derived measure is a noisy estimate of the true parameter, and (iii) the use of low-frequency data to create the estimates increases the measurement noise. It is well known that errors in the variables bias downward (towards zero) the estimated regression coefficients. This means that the effect of liquidity is hard to detect even when it exists and, further, this could aggrevate potential omitted-variable problems.

3.2 Equity markets

3.2.1 Cross-section tests

The effect of liquidity on asset pricing was first studied by Amihud and Mendelson (1986a), whose model produces two major empirical predictions (see Sections 2.2–2.3 above):

1. Expected asset return is an increasing function of illiquidity costs, and

38   Empirical Evidence

2. The relationship is concave due to the clientele effect (Section 2.3): In equilibrium, less liquid assets are allocated to investors with longer holding periods, which mitigates the compensation that they require for the costs of illiquidity.

These predictions are tested using stock returns over the period 1961–1980 and data on quoted bid–ask spreads for 1960–1979. The relative spread is the ratio of the dollar spread to the stock price, where the spread is the average of the beginning- and end-of-year end-of-day quotes, collected from Fitch quote sheets for NYSE and AMEX stocks. Every year, stocks are grouped into 49 (7 × 7) portfolios sorted on previous-year relative spread and within that, sorted on previously-estimated beta, and monthly return is calculated for each portfolio. The estimation is done by a pooled time-series and cross-section GLS regression which employs an estimation of the variance–covariance matrix of the 49 portfolios.

The estimation model is a regression of the portfolio monthly return on the portfolios' previously-estimated betas and previous-year average relative spreads. The spread effect is estimated in a piece-wise linear fashion, using dummy variables for the seven spread groups and the mean spread for each portfolio in each year. Thus, the regression explicitly accounts for the effect of the spread on (a) the level of the portfolio's average return and on (b) the slope of the return–spread relationship. The model's predictions are that (1) the portfolio return *increases* with the bid–ask spread, which is the main prediction, and (2) the return–spread slope *decreases* in the bid–ask spread, reflecting concavity.

The results support both predictions. The alternative hypotheses – that average return is not increasing in the spread, and that the slope is not decreasing in the spread – are rejected. The following illustrates the effect of the spread. From spread-portfolio 1 to spread-portfolio 4, the average spread increases by 0.659% and the monthly stock return increases by 0.242% (roughly 3% per annum), a ratio of 0.37. From portfolio 4 to 7, the spread rises by 2.063% and the average return rises by 0.439%, a ratio of 0.21. That is, the return–spread relationship for low-spread portfolios is nearly twice as high as it is for high-spread portfolios.

In addition, the model estimates the effect of the firm's size (capitalization) on stock return. The hypothesis is that if size reflects an aspect of liquidity – it is less costly to trade stocks of larger companies – then the size effect should weaken once the equation includes the bid–ask spread, which is a more direct measure of liquidity costs. Indeed, the bid–ask spread is known to be negatively related to firm size, as shown by Stoll and Whaley (1983) and others. The results support this prediction. The negative effect of size is weakened – it becomes insignificant – once the spread is included in the equation. Note, however, that the results could accommodate the size effect in addition to the effect of the bid–ask spread since the relative spread alone does not capture all aspects of liquidity.

A convenient summary of the results is provided in Amihud and Mendelson (1986b). Given the concave effect of the spread on expected return, the following model is estimated:

$$R_j = 0.0065 + 0.0010\beta_j + 0.0021 ln(S_j),$$

where R_j is the monthly stock portfolio return in excess of the 90-day Treasury bill rate, β_j is the systematic risk, estimated from data in the preceding period, and S_j is the relative bid–ask spread in relative bid–ask spread in the preceding year. All coefficients significant. By this estimation, the return difference between a stock with a 1.5% spread and a stock with 1% spread (and the same β) is 0.087% per month or roughly 1% per year. The return difference is greater – 0.15% per month (or 1.8% annually) for a stock with 1% spread compared to a same-risk stock with 0.5% spread.

The estimated return–spread relationship is illustrated in Figure 3.1.

Amihud and Mendelson (1989) further estimate the return–spread relationship, accounting also for the effect of volatility. Constantinides (Constantinides, 1986, see Section 2.6) shows that the effect of trading costs may be confounded with that of risk. While in Constantinides (1986) model, trading costs have only second-order effect on asset returns, expected return rises with volatility because higher volatility induces more frequent trading, which makes investors incur higher trading costs. Amihud and Mendelson thus add to the estimation model,

40   Empirical Evidence

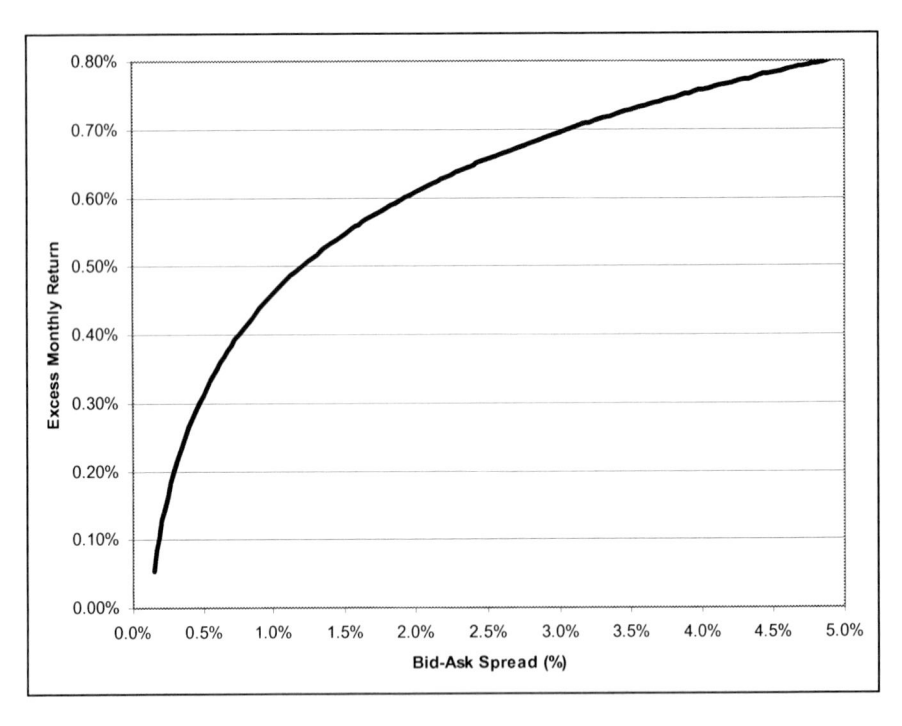

Fig. 3.1 Relationship between stocks' excess monthly returns and bid–ask spreads for a given level of systematic risk. Based on Amihud and Mendelson (1986b).

which includes the portfolio's beta and relative spread, the standard deviation of market-model residuals (unsystematic risk). The results show that while the bid–ask spread effect remains positive and significant, the effect of the unsystematic risk is generally negative but insignificantly different from zero.

For Nasdaq National Market System stocks, bid–ask spreads at the end of the day are available on the CRSP daily database, which facilitates the study of the return–spread relationship with more accurate data than in Amihud and Mendelson (1986b). Also, while on the NYSE and AMEX individual investors could trade through limit orders that had priority over the specialist's quotes and thus avoid the cost of the spread (though incurring the costs of risk and delay), on Nasdaq trading was done mostly through market makers, and investors had to incur the cost of the spread.[1] Consequently, the estimated effect of the bid–ask spread is expected to be stronger when using Nasdaq stocks. This is indeed the finding by Eleswarapu (1997), who estimates a model where the stock return is regressed on the stock's beta, relative spread, and log(size). The estimation is performed for individual stocks employing the Fama and MacBeth (1973) method. The only consistently significant effect is that of the relative spread, whose coefficient is positive and significant for both January and non-January months, whereas the coefficient of log(size) is negative and insignificant and that of beta is positive and significant only in January.[2] The liquidity effect in non-January months is inconsistent with an earlier finding by Eleswarapu and Reinganum (1993) that liquidity affects stock returns only in January. These authors replicate the Amihud–Mendelson study but employ the Fama–Macbeth method in the cross-section estimation and obtain that the bid–ask spread effect is significant only in the month of January but not in non-January months or in the year as a whole, and the size effect is never significant. Then, employing a looser data requirement that allows more small firms into the sample results again in the spread effect being significant only in the month of January but insignificant for the entire year, whereas the size effect is negative and significant both in January and in the entire year (but neither variable is significant in non-January months; the issue of the seasonality in the liquidity effect is revisited by Amihud (2002) and by Hasbrouck (2005), see below).

A finer measure of illiquidity is used by Brennan and Subrahmanyam (1996): Kyle (1985) λ (see Section 2.7), estimated from intraday trade and quote data. Brennan and Subrahmanyam estimate λ by regressing the trade-by-trade price change, Δp_t, on the signed transaction size, q_t. The slope coefficient from this regression[3] is Kyle's λ

---

[1] Until 1997, customer limit orders were not displayed in Nasdaq and were not incorporated in market-makers' quotes even when the limit price was better than the best displayed quote.
[2] The separation between January and non-January is due to the "January Effect": Small-firm stocks tend to outperform the market only in January. See Keim (1983).
[3] For these regressions, the authors use two models, one by Glosten and Harris (1988) and the other by Hasbrouck (1991) which mainly differ in the specification of the order

which measures the price impact of a unit of trade size, being larger for less liquid stock.[4] The regression model also includes $D_t - D_{t-1}$, where $D_t = 1$ for a buy transaction and $D_t = -1$ for a sell transaction. The coefficient of this differential, ψ, reflects the fixed cost of trading that is unrelated to the order size. The illiquidity variables that are used are the average of the marginal cost of trading, $C_q = \lambda q/P$, where q and P are the monthly averages of trade size and price, respectively (or $C_n = \lambda n/P$, where n is the monthly average of number of shares outstanding) and the relative fixed cost of trading, ψ/P. These cost variables are estimated for the years 1984 and 1988.

These measures of illiquidity are then used in a cross-section regression of monthly NYSE stock returns for the years 1984–1991. The estimations are performed using pooled time series and cross section GLS regressions, where the dependent variable is the monthly portfolio return. Portfolios are formed annually by sorting stocks into 25 (5 × 5) portfolios on size and within that on λ. In addition to the two liquidity cost variables, the regression model includes the three Fama and French (1993) factors: The market return index, the small-minus-big firm return indexes and the high-minus-low book-to-market return index. Thus, the returns are effectively the intercepts from the Fama–French three-index model.

The results show that C_q (or C_n) have a positive and significant effect on returns adjusted by the Fama–French factors, after controlling for firm size and price reciprocal. For example, the excess monthly return on the highest C_q quintile is 0.55% higher than the respective return on the lowest C_q quintile. In addition, C_q^2 (or C_n^2) have a negative and significant effect, consistent with the Amihud and Mendelson (1986a) clientele effect that generates an increasing and concave relationship between return and illiquidity costs. Further, both ψ/P and $(\psi/P)^2$ have positive and significant effects. While the positive sign of ψ/P is consistent with a positive illiquidity effect,

---

quantity: The latter uses residual transaction size obtained from a regression model. The results from the two models are qualitatively similar.

[4] In Kyle (1985), λ is an increasing function of the variance of information and a decreasing function of the variance of uninformed trading.

the positive coefficient of $(\psi/P)^2$ is inconsistent with the Amihud–Mendelson concavity prediction – instead, it suggests a convex illiquidity effect. When these finer measures of liquidity are used, both the bid–ask spread and the firm size become insignificant. In conclusion, Brennan and Subrahmanyam's results support the positive effect of illiquidity on expected stock returns.

As pointed out, liquidity is an elusive concept and is hard to measure. In addition, data such as bid–ask spread and intra-daily quotes and trades are hard to obtain. Even if such data are available, tests of asset pricing models require data that span a long periods of time to increase the power of the tests. Therefore, researchers often use alternative measures based on daily data on volume, shares outstanding and prices, which are available for most markets.

Brennan et al. (1998) use the stock's dollar trading volume as a measure of liquidity in a multi-factor asset pricing model, a version of the APT, where the stock's excess return is a function of the loadings of the stock return on the factors. The study uses excess returns from a factor model (using either the Connor and Korajczyk (1988) or the Fama and French (1993) approach), thus obtaining risk-adjusted returns. These risk-adjusted returns are regressed cross-sectionally on the stock's volume (in log) as well as on other characteristics: Size, book-to-market ratio, price, dividend yield and past returns (to capture the momentum effect). The study is performed using CRSP data for individual stocks over the period 1966–1995. As expected, the results show that volume has a negative and significant effect on risk-adjusted stock returns. Specifically, a one standard deviation increase in the dollar volume brings about a decline in the monthly excess return of 0.29% for Nasdaq stocks and 0.11% for NYSE/AMEX stocks.

Datar et al. (1998) use stock turnover (the ratio of stock volume to the number of shares outstanding) as a measure of liquidity. If in equilibrium less liquid stocks are allocated to investors with longer holding periods (Amihud and Mendelson, 1986b), or investors reduce their trading frequency of illiquid stocks (Constantinides, 1986), then even though liquidity is not directly observed, it can be inferred from the average holding period of the stock, which is the reciprocal of the stock turnover.[5] Datar et al. estimate the cross-section of NYSE stock returns (years: 1963–1991) on stock turnover, controlling for size, book-to-market ratio and beta, employing the Fama and MacBeth (1973) method. The prediction is that the longer the average holding period of the stock (which implies lower liquidity), or the lower the turnover, the higher the expected return. The results are consistent with this prediction: The cross section of stock returns is negatively related to stock turnover, with the effect being significant. The turnover coefficient was also negative and significant for each of the two subperiods. Similar results on the negative return–turnover relationship are obtained for the Tokyo Stock Exchange by Hu (1997).

Rouwenhorst (1999) examines the returns in 20 emerging markets over 10 or less years. Sorting each country's returns by turnover, he obtains no difference between high- and low-sorted returns. However, there are no controls for other variables, and the test period may be too short. He also finds that turnover is higher for small and high-beta firms; absent controls for size and risk in analyzing the return–turnover relationship,[6] there may be a confounding of the turnover effect with that of size and risk. Another study that uses turnover as a measure of liquidity is by Nguyen et al. (2005). They study the effect of turnover on stock returns in two ways, using 1970–2002 data. In one test, they use the intercepts from Fama and French (1993) three-factor model (the market and factors for size and book-to-market ratio) and aggregate them into 25 portfolios, obtained by sorting on size or book-to-market and within that on turnover. The average coefficients do not show a systematic relationship with the turnover portfolios, which is inconsistent with a liquidity effect. In the second test, Nguyen et al. perform a cross-section analysis using individual stocks (instead of portfolios), employing the Fama and MacBeth (1973) method with the GLS setup of Litzenberger and Ramaswamy (1979). Controlling for beta, size, book-to-market ratio or for beta and co-skewness with the market (to capture a skewness preference by investors), they find that

---

[5] Indeed, ? find a positive relationship across stocks between the bid–ask spread and the average holding period, defined as the reciprocal of turnover, after controlling for size.
[6] In Datar et al. (1998), using U.S. data, turnover alone was negatively related to return.

turnover has a negative and significant coefficient, which is consistent with the liquidity effect.

Amihud (2002) examines the effect of illiquidity on the cross-section of stock returns using an illiquidity measure that is related to Kyle (1985) price impact coefficient λ. The measure is called $ILLIQ = |R|/(P*VOL)$, where R is daily return, P is the closing daily price and VOL is the number of shares traded during the day. Intuitively, $ILLIQ$ reflects the relative price change that is induced by a given dollar volume. This ratio is averaged for each stock over a year to obtain the stock's $ILLIQ$ for that period.[7] (As discussed later, $ILLIQ$ varies over time.) The stock's $ILLIQ$ is then used in cross-section regressions of monthly individual stock returns on their prior-year $ILLIQ$ and other control variables: Beta, size, volatility, dividend yield and past returns (period: 1963–1996, NYSE stocks). The results show that $ILLIQ$ has a positive and significant effect on stock returns, as suggested by the theory. This effect is positive and significant both in January and in non-January months and over both sub-periods of the entire period.

Gottesman and Jacoby (2005) consider the effect of the firm's payout policy and investors' personal taxes on the relationship between expected return and bid–ask spread in the Amihud and Mendelson (1986a) framework. Stock repurchase is tax-advantaged compared to dividend but it incurs transaction costs, thus a wider bid–ask spread reduces its attractiveness. Investors maximize expected net return–after transaction cost and after tax. Gottesman and Jacoby obtain that while for dividend-paying stock, return is an increasing and concave function of the bid–ask spread, for stock repurchases the function is increasing and it may be convex or concave, depending on the mass of investors' holding-period clientele. They test the theory using data from Nasdaq during 1993–1999, when stock repurchases were far more popular than in the 1961–1980 period studied by Amihud and Mendelson. The results show that in general, the return–spread relationship is positive and concave (controlling for other characteristics). This pattern also holds in

---

[7] Hasbrouck (2005) estimates the cross-stock correlation between the Kyle's λ, estimated from intraday data aggregated into 5-minutes intervals, and ILLIQ. The Pearson (Spearman) correlation across stocks is 0.54 (0.76). The correlations are higher for $ILLIQ^{1/2}$ and for stock portfolios.

a subsample of firms that pay dividends and do not repurchase their stock, whereas in the subsample of firms that repurchase their stock and pay no dividend the return–spread relationship is positive and possibly convex, but for this group the results are not statistically significant.

The papers considered so far have used liquidity measures that are based on trading costs or investors' holding periods. Chalmers and Kadlec (1998) consider the effect of *amortized* spread, the product of the effective relative spread[8] and the stock's turnover (whose reciprocal gives the average holding period) on returns using annual data on NYSE/AMEX stocks over the period 1983–1992.[9] In the context of the simplest liquidity model (Proposition 1 of Section 2.2), the slope coefficient of a regression of expected return on the amortized spread should be 1. In the regression of Chalmers and Kadlec, controlling for size, book-to-market ratio and volatility, they find that the coefficient on amortized spread is positive and large, 7.9, and statistically significant with all the control variables (though insignificant in other specifications). This large coefficient, while supporting the positive effect of amortized transaction costs on stock returns, is larger than would be predicted by the simplest liquidity theory. This can possibly result from the omission of a relevant variable which is correlated with the amortized spread. For instance, the liquidity clientele effect on excess return $(r^{*j} - r^f)$ in Proposition 2 or the effect of liquidity risk described in Proposition 3.

Swan and Westerholm (2002) measure of the illiquidity of stocks relative to bonds is the difference in amortized bid–ask spread for stocks and bonds, deflated by unity minus the absolute value of the transaction cost elasticity with respect to turnover. The underlying model endogenizes trading, where investors trade until they are indifferent between trading further or not. Their estimation, using Finnish data for 1993–1998, shows that their measure of illiquidity has a strong positive effect on the cross-section of stock returns.

---

[8] The effective relative spread is the difference between a transaction price and the preceding mid-point of the bid–ask spread, divided by price.
[9] The annual sample consists of only ten time periods – a small number and a short sample compared to other studies.

The difficulty of obtaining reliable liquidity measures from low-frequency (daily) data is addressed by Hasbrouck (2005) who examines three measures from daily data and correlates them with measures obtained from high-frequency microstructure data. The Gibbs sampler estimates the effective cost of trading from the square root of the (negative of the) serial covariance of daily price changes (following Roll, 1985), but truncating the negative outcomes, where the extent of truncation is determined by a Bayesian estimation. The Gibbs sampler is highly correlated with the effective spread estimated from transaction and quote data. The other two are $ILLIQ^{1/2}$ and Pastor and Stambaugh (2003) γ that measures the return reversal in response to volume shocks, which is larger for less liquid stocks (see below). Hasbrouck then estimates the effects of these illiquidity measures on the cross-section of stock returns that are risk-adjusted by first employing the Fama and French (1993) three-factor model (following Brennan et al., 1998) (period: 1962–2003). The cross-sectional model that is estimated from monthly data using the Fama and MacBeth (1973) method, also includes market capitalization (in log) and past returns. The results show that both the Gibbs sampler and $ILLIQ^{1/2}$ have positive and significant effect on the cross-section of stock returns, with the effect being stronger for NYSE/AMEX stocks than for Nasdaq stocks. However, the estimated effect is not robust over January/non January time periods.

A problem that is revisited at this stage by Spiegel and Wang (2005) is the possible confounding between the effects of illiquidity and risk on stock returns. Given the strong positive relationship that they find between illiquidity and idiosyncratic risk[10] (the standard deviation of factor-model residuals), the estimated return–liquidity effects may be confounded with the positive relationship between return and idiosyncratic risk that obtains if investors are not well-diversified (see, e.g., Levy, 1978; Merton, 1987) or under the model of Constantinides (1986), where portfolio rebalancing is impeded by trading costs. The

---

[10] Inventory models of the bid–ask spread suggest a positive relationship between the bid–ask spread and risk, see Stoll (1978a,b). The positive relationship between the bid–ask spread and idiosyncratic risk is estimated by Benston and Hagerman (1974). See also (Amihud and Mendelson, 1987, Section VIII) on the positive relationship between idiosyncratic risk and the bid–ask spread.

risk variable, *EIDIO*, is the conditional idiosyncratic standard deviation of Fama and French (1993) three-factor model residuals, estimated by EGARCH. Spiegel and Wang estimate the effect of *EIDIO* and of some measures of liquidity on stocks' risk-adjusted returns (following Brennan et al., 1998) in a cross-sectional model (period: 1962–2003). The illiquidity measures are Hasbrouck (2005) Gibbs sampler, Amihud (2002) *ILLIQ* and Pastor and Stambaugh (2003) γ. The model also includes a measure of liquidity – trading volume in dollars and in logarithm (see Brennan et al., 1998) – as well as size (in log) and past returns, accounting for the momentum effect. The explanatory variables are lagged, reflecting the information investors had when making their investment decision. The results show that whereas the illiquidity variables have a positive and significant effect in a model without *EIDIO*, their effect becomes insignificant when EIDIO is included in the model, whereas the coefficient of *EIDIO* is positive and significant through all models. The coefficient of trading volume (particularly for NYSE/AMEX stocks), a measure of liquidity, is negative and significant in all models. The results highlight the problem of measuring illiquidity and disentangling it from other measures such as idiosyncratic risk.

All studies surveyed so far use historical returns to investigate the effects of liquidity on expected return. Clearly, realized return is a very noisy measure of expected return. Loderer and Roth (2005) depart from this method and investigate how stock *prices* are affected by liquidity. Clearly, controlling for future cash-flow growth and dividend payout, price is a measure of the expected return, and after controlling for risk, the results give the effect of liquidity on expected return. Loderer and Roth use data from the Swiss Stock Exchange for the years 1995–2001 and regress stock P/E, the price–earning ratio, on liquidity, measured by the relative bid–ask spread, after controlling for projected earnings growth obtained from analysts' reports, dividend payout ratio, risk and size (orthogonalized to the relative spread). The results show that the spread has a negative and significant effect on the cross-section of stock prices, as expected by the theory. A similar conclusion on the negative effect of illiquidity on stock prices is obtained when using trading volume as a measure of liquidity. The price discount is economically significant, being 12% for a median-spread stock compared to a zero-spread stock for the median year in the sample. Loderer and Roth replicate this methodology and examine the price discount, as a result of illiquidity, for Nasdaq stocks. The median discount there is 28% (for the median year).

3.2.2 Liquidity changes over time

If liquidity affects asset prices, it stands to reason that *changes* in liquidity should change asset prices (*ceteris paribus*). This hypothesis is examined by Amihud et al. (1990). They suggest that the stock market crash of October 19, 1987 can be partly explained by a decline in investors' perception of the market's liquidity. At the time, a popular investment strategy was "portfolio insurance," by which stockholdings are reduced when prices fall and increased when prices rise. In an infinitely liquid market, such a strategy would have no impact on prices even when exercised by many investors. However, in the days prior to the crash there were massive stock sales and price declines, which may have caused investors to adjust downward their beliefs about market liquidity. Liquidity asset pricing theory implies that a downward revision in liquidity should cause a decline in stock prices. Amihud, Mendelson and Wood test this hypothesis as follows. They regress cross-sectionally the risk-adjusted returns of NYSE stocks that are included in the S&P 500 index on October 19, 1987 on the change in liquidity during that day, measured by the average daily bid–ask spread or by depth (the number of shares that could be traded at the quoted bid and ask prices). The results show that stocks that suffered the greatest decline in liquidity on that day also suffered the greatest decline in prices. Further, stocks whose liquidity recovered more by the end of the month (October 30, 1987) also enjoyed a greater recovery in price.

A well-controlled case of changes in stock liquidity is the case of transfer of stocks in the Tel Aviv Stock Exchange from a once-a-day call auction to semi-continuous trading. Stocks were transferred in batches, an average of 7 stocks in each, at random times over the years 1987–1994, without company discretion – all transfer decisions were made by the Exchange. This avoids the self-selection problem that arises when stocks transfer voluntarily from one trading system to another, such as moving from the Nasdaq to the NYSE or AMEX (see below), which may reflect private information. This case is also different from the cases in European exchanges where an entire market, or most of it, was transferred from an auction market to continuous trading.

Stocks that were transferred to the semi-continuous trading system obviously enjoyed greater liquidity in general. Amihud et al. (1997) find that their trading volume increased significantly relative to the market's and their liquidity ratio (the ratio of average absolute daily return to average daily dollar volume) declined. Consequently, the prices of the transferred stocks rose by at least 5%–6% and remained high. Cross-sectionally, the price increase was greater for stocks that enjoyed a greater increase in liquidity. Moreover, there was a liquidity externality: The prices of closely-related stocks (stocks of the same company with different voting rights) that were not transferred also rose, although by less.

Similar results are obtained by Muscarella and Piwowar (2001) for the Paris Bourse's transfer of stocks from a call to a continuous market, and by Kalay et al. (2002) for a later improvement in the trading system at the Tel Aviv Stock Exchange. In both studies, stocks that were transferred to a more liquid trading system enjoyed an increase in prices. Interestingly, Muscarella and Piwowar as well as Lauterbach (2001) find that some thinly-traded stocks that are transferred from the call to the continuous market realize a decline in liquidity and a decline in price. Lauterbach finds that the price decline is positively associated with a decline in relative trading volume that measures liquidity. Stocks that were immediately returned to the call market realized both a price increase and a rise in liquidity. This suggests that for thinly-traded stocks, a call auction may be an efficient mechanism to consolidate trading which contributes to liquidity and value, and further reinforces the positive relationship between liquidity and stock prices.[11]

---

[11] If the estimated price increase when stocks were transferred to a continuous market was due to some reason other than the increase in liquidity, this would likely result in the opposite price pattern.

In another study on the effect of changes in the trading environment on stock prices, Berkman and Eleswarapu (1998) examined the effect of changes in the forward trading facility (*Badla*) for 91 stocks on the Bombay Stock Exchange – the abolition on 12/1993 and the reinstatement on 3/1994. The *Badla* enables trading without affecting delivery, which was attractive to short-term traders. When it was abolished, the liquidity of the affected stocks declined sharply and their price fell by about 15% compared to the price of non-*Badla* stocks. In a cross-section analysis, Berkman and Eleswarapu find the decline in prices of *Badla* stocks was significantly associated with the decline in their liquidity (controlling for the change in volatility).

Exogenous changes in stock liquidity occur when the composition of the S&P 500 index changes. Stocks included in the index are subject to a great deal of trading that is not based on stock-specific information, such as by index funds and by hedgers of index futures and index options. Thus, including the stocks in the S&P 500 index increases their liquidity. It has been documented that stocks that join the index enjoy a price increase whereas those that are deleted suffer a price decline. These changes have been attributed to demand pressures. Hegde and McDermott (2003) document increases in the liquidity of stocks that are added to the S&P 500 index, with liquidity being measured in a number of ways: bid–ask spread (quoted and effective), volume, trading frequency, and the estimated parameters from Kyle's model, $\lambda n/P$ and particularly ψ/P (see above under the analysis of Brennan and Subrahmanyam, 1996). For deleted stocks, they find a decline in liquidity although the results are weaker since deletions are very noisy events. The authors then test in a cross-section regression the hypothesis that the price changes of these stocks are related to changes in their liquidity, measured by direct information cost. They find that the price increase of added stocks is positively and significantly associated with the improvement in liquidity.

Exchange listing generally induces improvement in liquidity and an increase in price. However, being voluntary, it may reflect self-selection due to favorable information. Kadlec and McConnell (1994) and Elyasiani et al. (2000) examine the effect of listing on both stock value and stock liquidity. The respective samples are 273 stocks that listed on the NYSE during 1980–1989 and 895 listings on NYSE and AMEX between 1971 and 1994. Both studies find that listing brought about a significant increase in stock price and at the same time a significant decline in the bid–ask spread. In a cross-section analysis, the studies find that price changes are negatively associated with changes in the spread, as would be predicted if liquidity enhances value. (In addition, the studies control for the change in number of shareholders and change in volatility). Bollen and Whaley (2004) too find that stocks that transferred from Nasdaq to the NYSE enjoyed greater liquidity and an increase in price, and they include controls to overcome the self-selection problem.

When a stock is delisted from an exchange, its liquidity dramatically declines. Involuntary delisting occurs because of violations of listing requirements, and the delisted stocks are subsequently traded in less liquid markets. Since delisting is involuntary, the delisting event per se does not convey new private information, and thus any observed price effect on the delisting day reflects the effect of the change in liquidity due to the change in the stock's trading arena. Angel et al. (2005) examine stocks that are involuntarily delisted from the Nasdaq Stock Market and are subsequently traded in the OTC Bulletin Board and in the Pink Sheets. They find a large and significant deterioration in liquidity, measured by trading volume, number of quotes per day and the bid–ask spread, and a large and significant price decline, about 18%, around the delisting day. This price decline understates the total effect of delisting because the event was partly anticipated. Similar results are obtained by Macey and O'Hara (2005) for 55 stocks that were delisted from the NYSE. For a sub-sample of 12 large stocks they find that stock prices fell along with a decline in trading volume and an increase in the percent bid–ask spread (the dollar bid–ask spread declined).[12]

Some corporate events may change the liquidity of the firm's stock and, if liquidity is priced, they can affect the stock price. Amihud et al.

---

[12] Delisting, however, while involuntary, may not be totally beyond the firm's control. Reasons for delisting include the stock price being below some minimum, too little ownership dispersion and delinquency in meeting SEC filing requirements. These problems can be rectified by the firm if it chooses. If it fails to do so, the delisting that ensues due to these reasons may reflect information and ought to be treated separately.

(1999) study a case where companies in Japan reduced the minimum trading unit of their stock and consequently increased the number of their individual shareholders. The greater breath of ownership led to significant increases in stock liquidity and in stock prices.[13] Amihud et al. (2003) examine the increase in stock liquidity that follows the exercise of outstanding stock warrants, which increases the stock's float without changing anything else in the firm. They find that this led to a decline in stock illiquidity (measured by Roll's (1985) bid–ask spread) and that stock prices abnormal returns being positively and significantly associated with the improvement in liquidity.

The time series effect of market-wide changes in stock liquidity on stock prices is examined by Amihud (2002) and Jones (2002). Amihud proposes that (i) expected stock return for period $t + 1$ is an increasing function of illiquidity for $t + 1$ as expected in period t, and (ii) an unexpected rise in illiquidity in period t lowers stock prices in the same period, producing a negative returns – unexpected liquidity relationship, consistent with the theoretical results in Acharya and Pedersen (Acharya and Pedersen 2005; see Proposition 4 in Section 2.4). To test these hypotheses, Amihud constructs a measure of aggregate illiquidity, $AILLIQ$ (the average of stocks' $ILLIQ$, the daily ratio of absolute return to dollar volume), for NYSE stocks between 1962 and 1997. He finds that average stock excess return (monthly or annual) is an increasing function of lagged $AILLIQ$, which measures expected illiquidity ($AILLIQ$ is highly autoregressive), and is a decreasing function of contemporaneous unexpected $AILLIQ$ (the residual from an autoregressive model of $AILLIQ$). Both results are consistent with the liquidity theory of asset pricing.

Amihud further proposes that both effects of illiquidity should be stronger for less-liquid stocks. Liquid stocks, while being subject to the same effects, become more attractive when liquidity worsens – a "flight to liquidity" – which mitigates the negative effects of increased illiquidity. The results support this hypothesis. The negative effect on returns of market liquidity shocks, and the positive effect of lagged

---

[13] The positive effect of increased ownership breath on stock price can also be explained by Merton (1987) model.

illiquidity on subsequent return, are both stronger for smaller firms, with the effect being monotonic in size, suggesting that the exposure to liquidity shocks is greater for less liquid stocks.

Jones (2002) examines the time series effects of market liquidity on stock prices over the twentieth century. He uses two measures of liquidity: transaction costs, measured by bid–ask spread and brokerage fees on the Dow Jones component stocks, and stock turnover. Jones finds that stock returns can be predicted a year or more ahead: High spreads predict high stock returns and high turnover predicts low stock returns.

The time-series liquidity-expected return relationship is further studied by Bekaert et al. (2005) using data from 19 emerging markets and the U.S. (which proxies the world index) and employing a VAR analysis. The measure of illiquidity used is the relative number of days of zero returns in each stock, averaged over all stocks used for the country index. This follows Lesmond et al. (1999) who suggest that higher transaction costs reduce the likelihood of trading for a given information signal. Indeed, the authors find that this measure (or a related measure of no-trade days) is highly correlated with other measures of illiquidity for U.S. data. The results show that (a) liquidity predicts return (monthly data) with the effect being negative, and (b) unexpected liquidity is positively correlated with contemporaneous returns. Both results are consistent with those of Amihud (2002) and Proposition 4 in Section 2.4. The results are qualitatively similar when returns are replaced by dividend yield. The use of data from emerging markets enables also to examine the effect of liquidity on stock returns when the market is closed to foreign investors and when it is opened up, the latter being measured by foreign investors' holdings relative to the market capitalization. The estimations then show that opening up a country's capital market to foreign investors reduces the effect (i.e., the coefficient) of liquidity on stock returns.

3.2.3 Pricing of liquidity risk

The studies reviewed in Section 2.2 examine the effects of the *level* of liquidity on stock returns. Since liquidity varies over time, as documented in Hasbrouck and Seppi (2001), Huberman and Halka (2001), Amihud (2002), and Chordia et al. (2002), it stands to reason that liquidity *risk* should also be priced.

Pastor and Stambaugh (2003) propose that asset prices should reflect a premium for the sensitivity of stock returns to market-wide liquidity: Stocks with greater exposure to market liquidity shocks – i.e., with greater systematic liquidity risk – should earn higher returns.

Pastor and Stambaugh's market liquidity measure is based on Campbell et al. (1993) observation that in a regression of a stock's daily return on its signed lagged dollar volume, the coefficient which captures the bounce in the stock price following a given trading volume is more negative for less liquid stocks. Pastor and Stambaugh perform monthly estimations of the following model for each stock j:

$$r^e_{j,d+1} = \theta_j + \varphi_j r_d + \gamma_j \text{sign}(r^e_{j,d}) \cdot v_{j,d} + e_{j,d+1}, \qquad (3.1)$$

where $r^e_{j,d}$ is the return on stock j on day d in excess of the market return and $v_{j,d}$ is the daily dollar volume.[14] Stocks with more negative γ_j are interpreted as less liquid.[15] The market's liquidity for month t, γ_t, is the average of the individual stocks' $\gamma_{j,t}$. Finally, the liquidity measure L_t is the residual from an AR1 model of $\Delta\gamma_t = \gamma_t - \gamma_{t-1}$ (adjusted for variations in market capitalization over time), and it is serially uncorrelated. The stock's exposure to liquidity shocks is β^L, the regression coefficient of the stock returns on L_t, with the model also including the three Fama and French (1993) factors. The study eventually uses the predicted β^L, which is a function of seven stock characteristics,[16] or historical values of β^L. The data are for NYSE, AMEX and Nasdaq over the period 1966–1999.

If liquidity risk is priced, stock returns should be increasing in their liquidity beta β^L. Pastor and Stambaugh sort stocks in each year by their predicted β^L (based on historical β^L and other stock characteristics) and aggregate them into 10 portfolios. The return series of these

---

[14] On a day of zero stock return, the volume obtains the sign of the market return.
[15] Pastor and Stambaugh find that γ_j increases in firm size, as expected if γ_j measures liquidity. However, Hasbrouck (2005) finds a small and unstable correlation between γ_j and a measure of Kyle's λ_j that is estimated from microstructure data.
[16] The characteristics with the most stable effect over time (and the sign of their coefficients) are historical beta (+), return volatility (−) and price (+).

portfolios are then linked over time to form a time series of returns, which are used to estimate portfolio alphas from the market model or from Fama–French three- or four-factors model. Pastor and Stambaugh find that these portfolio alphas are increasing over the 10 beta portfolios which are ranked from low to high β^L. That is, the expected return is an increasing function of the stock's sensitivity to market-wide liquidity shocks, which means that liquidity *risk* is priced.

Acharya and Pedersen (2005) study a broad model of pricing liquidity level and liquidity risk. Expected excess return over the risk-free rate, $E(r^e_{j,t+1})$, is a function of both the expected illiquidity, $E(c_{j,t+1})$, and four systematic risk variables: the ordinary return beta $\beta = \text{cov}(r_j, r_m)/\text{var}(r_m - c_m)$ and three liquidity-related betas, $\beta^{L1} = \text{cov}(c_j, c_m)/\text{var}(r_m - c_m)$, $\beta^{L2} = \text{cov}(r_j, c_m)/\text{var}(r_m - c_m)$ and $\beta^{L3} = \text{cov}(c_j, r_m)/\text{var}(r_m - c_m)$, where c_j and c_m are the illiquidity cost of stock j and of the market, respectively (see Section 2 above). The (unconditional version of the) model is:

$$E\left(r^i_{t+1}\right) = r^f + \kappa E\left(c^i_{t+1}\right) + \lambda\left(\beta + \beta^{L1} - \beta^{L2} - \beta^{L3}\right) \quad (3.2)$$

where κ adjusts for the difference between the average holding period and the monthly estimation period. The liquidity risk β^{L2} is analogous to that used by Pastor and Stambaugh (2003).

The empirical estimation of the model employs as a measure of illiquidity Amihud (2002) *ILLIQ*, calculated from daily CRSP returns and volume for NYSE/AMEX stocks for the period 1964–1999. Stocks are sorted every year by their *ILLIQ* or by their size and grouped into 25 portfolios. The monthly illiquidity of each portfolio and of the market is calculated as the residual from an autoregressive model of the portfolio (average) *ILLIQ*, adjusted for market capitalization. The four portfolio betas are estimated from the monthly data over the entire period. Naturally, β is higher for less liquid stocks. As for the three liquidity betas, illiquid stocks have higher β^{L1} and more negative β^{L2} and β^{L3}. Thus, the absolute values of the liquidity betas – the measures of exposure to liquidity risk – are greater for less liquid stock. The higher liquidity risk of illiquid stocks is consistent with the notion of "flight to quality" or "flight to liquidity": in times of liquidity crisis, the illiquid securities suffer the most.

Model (3.2) is estimated using GMM and the results show that the excess return is positively and significantly related to the portfolio's $\beta_{net} = \beta + \beta^{L1} - \beta^{L2} - \beta^{L3}$ as well as to its level of illiquidity $E(c)$. The model's explanatory power in the cross-section is higher than the standard CAPM. Indeed, the liquidity-adjusted CAPM fairs better in specification tests and has a higher R^2.

To test the effect of liquidity risk over and above the effects of market risk and liquidity level, the authors estimate

$$E\left(r_{t+1}^i\right) = r^f + \kappa E\left(c_{t+1}^i\right) + \lambda^1 \beta + \lambda^2 \left(\beta^{L1} - \beta^{L2} - \beta^{L3}\right)$$

The estimated coefficient on liquidity risk λ^2 is positive and significant in several, but not all, specifications. This is consistent with liquidity risk being priced.

Finally, Acharya and Pedersen assess the relative economic significance of liquidity level and liquidity risk by considering the return premium required to hold the most illiquid stocks rather than the liquid ones. Under the restriction of one risk premium λ and with κ calibrated to the average turnover, the total annual liquidity risk premium is estimated to 1.1% while the premium for liquidity level is 3.5%. When the risk premium on each kind of liquidity risk is estimated freely, the effect of liquidity risk rises, but the statistical significance is limited. Pastor and Stambaugh (2003) find a larger effect of liquidity risk, but they do not control for liquidity level.

Another specification of a model with systematic liquidity risk is proposed by Martinez et al. (2005). Beginning with the pricing kernel $E_{t-1}[M_t(1 + R_{j,t})]$, they assume that $M_t = d_{0,t-1} + d_{1,t-1} r_{m,t} + d_{2,t-1} L_t$, where L_t is a replicating liquidity portfolio, and $d_{k,t} = d_{k,0} + d_{k,1} bm_t$ for $k = 0, 1, 2$, with bm_t being the book-to-market ratio. This gives rise to the asset pricing model

$$E(r_j) = c_0 + c_1 \beta_{j,m} + c_2 \beta_{j,bm} + c_3 \beta_{j,mbm} + c_4 \beta_{j,L} + c_5 \beta_{j,Lbm}, \quad (3.3)$$

where $\beta_{j,x} = \text{cov}(r_{j,t}, x_t)/\text{var}(x_t)$ and $\beta_{j,xbm} = \text{cov}(r_{j,t}, bm_{t-1} x_t)/\text{var}(bm_{t-1} x_t)$ for $x = r_m$ or L. It is expected that $\beta_{j,L} < 0$ and $\beta_{j,Lmb} < 0$. Notably, $\beta_{j,L}$ is related to Pastor and Stambaugh's liquidity beta and to Acharya and Pedersen (2005) β^{L2}. The focus of the test is on whether liquidity is priced, i.e., whether c_4 and c_5 are significantly different from zero.

For the factor L, the study uses three measures of liquidity: Pastor and Stambaugh (2003) market liquidity, Amihud (2002) $ILLIQ$ and the return differential between portfolios of stocks with high and low sensitivity to changes in their relative bid–ask spread. The data are obtained from the Spanish stock market for the years 1993–2000. The results show that when L is measured as $ILLIQ$, the coefficients c_4 and c_5 are negative and significant, that is, higher (absolute) liquidity-related betas lead to higher expected returns.

The pricing of liquidity risk in nineteen emerging markets is studied by Bekaert et al. (2005) in a model that extends Acharya and Pedersen (2005). They model the effects of liquidity factors – both a country and a global (U.S.-based) factor, as well as a country and a global (U.S.) return factor, allowing for different prices for the two risks, market and liquidity. Further, their model enables to study the differences in the effects on expected return of segmented and integrated markets, with the difference being whether or not the risks due to the global return and liquidity factors are present. The results show that while the price of the local market risk is not significant, the price of local liquidity risk is positive and significant. The positive and significant effect of the local liquidity risk is preserved in a mixed model that allows for both segmentation and integration. In the latter model, the price of global liquidity risk is positive but only marginally significant (the same applies to the pricing of the global return factor). The best fitting model assumes a locally-segmented market and estimates a compensation for local liquidity risk of 85 basis points per month.[17] This suggests that opening up the local market to foreign investors does not eliminate the effect of local liquidity risk, which remains the most important priced factor.

Sadka (2003) examines the pricing of liquidity risk in a factor model that includes the three Fama–French factors and a liquidity factor L, calculated as an average of the stocks' permanent market impact

---

[17] In this model, the estimated effect of the level of liquidity on expected return is positive, which is contrary to theory.

coefficient. This coefficient is similar to Kyle's λ as estimated by Glosten and Harris (1988) but it separates permanent from transitory price impact effects, and the measure that is eventually used reflects only the permanent price impact (period: 1983–2001). For each portfolio, formed based on a 5 × 5 momentum/liquidity sorting or size/book-to-market sorting, the factor loadings (β coefficients) are estimated in a model that includes L and the three Fama–French factors. Notably, the β coefficient of factor L is related Acharya and Pedersen (2005) β^{L2}. Finally, the asset pricing relationship is estimated by a cross-section regression of monthly returns on the factor loadings, employing the Fama and MacBeth (1973) method. The results show that the liquidity factor is priced, with a positive risk premium, whereas the other factors are not. This supports the importance of liquidity risk in asset pricing. However, Sadka reports that the return on high-minus-low price impact is statistically insignificant, which is inconsistent with the results of Brennan and Subrahmanyam (1996). This may be due to the use of different measures of price impact or a different study period.

Fujimoto and Watanabe (2005) propose that the effects on stock returns of liquidity – both level and risk – on stock returns varies over time across identifiable states. They estimate the liquidity beta from a regression of portfolio return on a liquidity index (the negative of the residuals of an AR(2) model of modified $ILLIQ$) by a regime-switching model. This liquidity beta is analogous to that in Pastor and Stambaugh (2003) and to β^{L2} in Acharya and Pedersen (2005). Fujimoto and Watanabe find that the liquidity betas are higher – for both large and small firm portfolios – in states when investors may expect liquidity needs, especially when turnover is abnormally high.[18] The high liquidity-beta states are identified to be during 43–47 months (depending on the portfolio sorting method) out of the 480 months of the study period, 1965–2004. They subsequently find that in states of high liquidity betas, there is a greater effect on stock returns of the level of liquidity and of the price of liquidity risk (measured by the coefficients of the liquidity betas).

---

[18] The study identifies other variables that indicate liquidity needs. The liquidity beta is also high in states of high volatility, high probability of recession, low growth of the index of leading indicators and low consumer expectations.

Whereas all previous studies used a measure of liquidity as a factor, Liu (2004b) uses a factor-mimicking stock portfolio that reflects the liquidity premium, constructed in a similar way to the Fama–French SMB and HML factors. Liu measures stock illiquidity in each month as the sum of the number of no-trading days and the average reciprocal of daily turnover (scaled) over the prior 250 trading days. Illiquid stocks have both more non-trading day and higher value of the reciprocal of turnover, which proxies the stock's holding period (see Amihud and Mendelson, 1986a; Datar et al., 1998). Stocks are then sorted by this illiquidity measure into 10 portfolios. The sample includes NYSE, AMEX and Nasdaq stocks over 41 years, 1963–2003. The results are that return alphas from the Fama–French model increase almost monotonically in the rank of illiquidity, with the difference in alphas between high and low illiquidity being significant. Liu's novel construction of a factor-mimicking portfolio of high-minus-low illiquidity reinforces the earlier results: Liquidity risk is priced. Liu then proposes a model with only two factors: excess market return and the illiquidity factor. The alphas from this model are not significantly related to stock size or to book-to-market ratio, supporting the adequacy of the liquidity-based two-factor asset pricing model. This model also renders the momentum effect insignificant after adjusting for trading costs.

Another form of liquidity risk is studied by Chordia et al. (2001) who extend the Brennan et al. (1998) approach to estimate a model of cross-sectional risk-adjusted returns on stock characteristics. As liquidity they use trading activity measured either as dollar trading volume (as in Brennan et al., 1998) or turnover (as in Datar et al., 1998). A novel aspect of their analysis is the inclusion of the volatility of trading activity. The results show that both the level and volatility of trading activity have a negative and significant effect on risk-adjusted stock returns. Their finding that investors demand a compensation for liquidity volatility is contrary to the authors' initial hypothesis. The authors suggest that the effect of liquidity volatility may be due to its correlation with some omitted and unknown risk factor. Alternatively, volatility in trading activity may imply larger investor following which, by Merton (1987), should lead to lower expected return. Yet another hypothesis would be that liquidity volatility could be helpful to investors if they can choose to trade when liquidity is favorable. The finding of Chordia et al. is not directly comparable to the above studies by Pastor and Stambaugh (2003) and Acharya and Pedersen (2005) that focus on systematic liquidity risk, not total volatility.

The above papers study the effects of liquidity costs which result in part from asymmetric information (see Section 2.7 above). Easley et al. (2002) suggest that information risk affects asset returns since asymmetric information exposes uninformed investors to the risk of being unable to infer information from prices, and this risk is priced. They test this hypothesis on the cross-section of asset returns, employing their measure PIN, the probability of informed trading, estimated by maximum likelihood from a structural model, following Easley et al. (1997). PIN is an estimate of the fraction of information-based orders, based on the imbalance between buy and sell trades. They indeed find that across stocks, PIN is negatively correlated with size and positively correlated with the bid–ask spread. Using data for NYSE stocks over the years 1983–1998, the effect of PIN is examined in a cross-section regression of stock returns with controls for beta, size and book-to-market ratio, employing the methods of Fama and MacBeth (1973) and Litzenberger and Ramaswamy (1979). The results show that PIN has a positive and significant coefficient. The positive effect of PIN survives when other variables – bid–ask spread, return standard deviation, turnover and the coefficient of variation of turnover – are included in the equation. In a multiple regression, the liquidity measures have the expected signs (positive for the bid–ask spread, negative for turnover), yet the positive and significant effect of PIN means that it contains information beyond other liquidity-related variables. (The paper finds some puzzling results for the spread in certain specifications.) The results thus suggest that the risk of informed trading is priced.

3.2.4 Restricted stock

The *existence* of a liquidity effect may be tested directly by comparing two assets that are identical in every respect except in their liquidity.

As pointed out in the introduction to this section, the price difference between such two assets can be attributed to the effect of liquidity. This is the case with restricted stocks. In the United States, restricted or "letter" stocks that are issued by publicly-traded companies are not registered with the SEC for trading in public markets,[19] but they can sometimes be traded privately, and the private transaction prices are reported to the SEC. Until 1990, the SEC required that restricted stocks would not be traded in the public markets for at least two years after issuance. Thereafter, the holder could sell the stock in the public market subject to some restrictions, and block sales of restricted stocks following the 2-year period required registration with the SEC. In 1990, the SEC dropped the registration requirement for block sales and in 1997 it lowered the minimum holding period from two years to one year, which consequently increased the liquidity of restricted stocks.

The 1971 *Institutional Investor Study* conducted by the SEC examines the discounts on 398 letter stock transactions over the 1966–1969 period compared to their publicly-traded counterparts. The study finds a mean discount of 26% and a median discount of 24%, with smaller companies associated on average with larger discounts. Gelman (1972) studies the prices of restricted stocks purchased by investment companies that specialized in the purchase of such stock using 89 transactions over the 1968–1970 period and finds a mean and median discount of 33%. Trout (1977, study period 1968–1972, 60 transactions) finds an average discount of 33%, and Maher (1976, study period 1969–1973, 34 transactions) finds restricted stock discount of 35% (both mean and median). Solberg (1979) analyzes the discounts approved by courts (based on a number of underlying studies) for the lower marketability of restricted stock, finding a median discount of 39%.

Silber (1991) studies 69 restricted stock issues over the 1981–88 period, finding a mean discount of 34%. Silber also finds that the discount is an increasing function of the size of the restricted block transaction relative to the total common stock, and a decreasing function of the company's size and its profitability, controlling for special relationship

---

[19] Such stocks may be issued when a public firm raises private capital or as part of an acquisition. Restricted stocks may also be held by company founders or insiders who are prohibited from selling their shares in the open market for a period of time.

between the company and the restricted stock holder. That is, greater liquidity of the traded shares generates a positive externality on the value of the restricted stock (see also Amihud et al., 1997), and the discount is greater for "problem firms" (with low profitability).

Generally, restricted stock discounts over the pre-1990 period were around 1/3 of the value of the equivalent – but publicly traded–stock. Post-1997 studies find similar behavior but lower discounts ranging between 13% and 21%, consistent with the less-stringent restrictions on restricted stock during the later period (Pratt, 2003). To illustrate the meaning of a discount of 1/3 of value in terms of excess return, consider the following. Assume that the annual return on the publicly-traded stock is 10%, and that the restriction period is 2.5 years (including restrictions on the rate of unwinding the position). Then, the annual excess return due to the illiquidity of the restricted stock is 19%.

The value effect of restrictions on trading is studied by Chen and Xiong (2001) for restricted stocks in China. There, a typical listed company has, in addition to its traded stock, two classes of restricted stock: Institutional stocks that can be transferred only in irregularly scheduled auctions and state shares that are only privately transferable. The study obtains data on auction prices of institutional shares and the prices of private transactions for the state shares. Chen and Xiong find that the discounts on the two types of restricted shares compared to their publicly-traded counterparts is 78% and 86%, respectively. As in Silber (1991), the illiquidity discount decreases in the firm's size (measured by book value) and increases if it has problems, such as a low price-to-book ratio. The discount also declines in the firm's age.

3.3 Fixed-income markets

The fixed income markets provide a fruitful area for examining the effects of liquidity on asset prices, since the cash flows for fixed-income instruments are typically known with greater certainty than in the case of stocks. Studies of the effects of liquidity on bonds examine the effect of liquidity on the bond's yield to maturity, which – for riskless bonds, such as government securities – measures the expected return if the bond is held to maturity. For corporate bonds which can default, the yield to maturity after controlling for the effect of default provides a low-noise estimate of the expected return, compared to the case of stocks where realized returns are used to estimate expected returns.

3.3.1 U.S. treasury securities

A key advantage of using U.S. Treasury securities is that they are risk-free, thus it is unnecessary to separate the default premium from a liquidity premium, as is the case with corporate bonds. This provides relatively "clean" tests of the effects of liquidity on bond yields (although one must be mindful of repo and tax effects as discussed below). Amihud and Mendelson (1991a) directly test the effect of bond liquidity on yields, without the need to control for risk. They compare the yields on Treasury notes and bills with the *same* time to maturity. With less than six months to maturity, both are discount instruments with identical payoffs. However, the two instruments are traded in different markets with bills being far more liquid. This is because notes with a short time left to maturity are "off-the-run," having been issued long ago and locked in investors' portfolios, whereas bills are issued frequently for short maturities and are actively traded throughout their life, being effectively "on-the-run" instruments. The brokerage fee per $1 million was $12.50–$25 for bills compared with 78\frac{1}{8}$ for notes; bid–ask spreads for bills were of the order of $$\frac{1}{128}$ compared to $$\frac{1}{32}$ for notes, both per $100 face value; and the search for a counterparty for notes took significantly longer than for bills. This gives rise to the hypothesis that bills should have a lower yield to maturity than notes with the same time to maturity.

The hypothesis is tested on the yield differential of 489 pairs of notes and bills with less than 6 months to maturity over 37 trading days during the period April–November 1987, using actual quotes "pulled off the screen." The pairs are constructed by matching a note with bills whose maturities straddled the note's. The average bid–ask spread on the notes and bills are, respectively, 3 basis points and 0.78 basis point. The average note yield is 6.52% compared to 6.09% for the bills, a difference of 43 basis points, which is significant both economically and statistically. This suggests a yield premium due to illiquidity.[20] In addition, given the higher fixed cost of trading notes, Amihud and Mendelson hypothesize that the yield differential should be larger for shorter maturities. They indeed find that the notes–bills yield differential is increasing in the reciprocal of the time to maturity. The notes–bills yield differential is also found to be declining in the note's coupon, reflecting constraints on some institutions to distribute only accrued interest. This liquidity constraints on these institutions makes them pay a premium for the liquidity afforded by the notes' coupon.

It would seem that the notes–bills yield differential provides a profitable and riskless arbitrage opportunity: buy the high-yield note and short a similar-maturity low-yield bill, holding them to maturity. However, this exercise ignores the very essence of the illiquidity: Arbitrage trades also entail transaction costs. Amihud and Mendelson simulate this arbitrage transaction, taking into account the associated transaction costs: The bid–ask spread, brokerage fees and cost of carrying the short position. At the end, the apparent arbitrage profit disappears (it is insignificantly different from zero). This suggests that the price differential between securities of different liquidity is bounded by arbitrage.

Kamara (1994) studies the determinants of the yield differentials for matched-maturity note–bill pairs using 91 observations of bid and ask prices for Treasury bills and notes with about 14 weeks to maturity over the period January 1977–July 1984. He posits that the notes–bills yield differential reflects differences in liquidity, tax treatment and dealer inventories. Kamara proposes to measure the liquidity difference between notes and bills as the product of the volatility of the underlying rate (estimated from a GARCH model) by the ratio of the bills' turnover to the notes' turnover, where turnover is calculated using the ratio of dealer transactions to the absolute value of their net positions. This measure of "liquidity risk" of a trade reflects the variance of the security's value between the point in time when a trader wishes to trade and the point when she actually trades (Garbade and Silber, 1979;

---

[20] A similar observation on the yield differential between notes and bills is made by Garbade (1984). The notes-bills difference has considerably shrunk recently (Strebulaev, 2002), which may be attributed at least in part to structural changes in the fixed-income market.

Mendelson, 1982). This variance is proportional to the time needed to find a counterparty and execute the transaction, and to the security's underlying return volatility. Since the average time to transact is not available, the turnover ratio is used as a proxy for the time ratio.

Kamara finds an average notes–bills bid yield differential of 34 basis points, a statistically and economically significant difference. The notes–bills bid yield differential is found to be increasing in the liquidity risk, supporting the role of liquidity in the pricing of bonds, as in (Amihud and Mendelson, 1991). In addition, Kamara finds a significant tax effect, reflecting the asymmetric tax treatment of notes priced above par value vs. notes priced below par value, and a transient effect of dealers' inventories: An increase in dealers' inventories of notes, which are the less-liquid asset, reduces the notes–bills yield differential.[21]

While Amihud and Mendelson (1991a) and Kamara (1994) compare "on-" and "off-the-run" short-term U.S. Treasury securities, other studies examine this issue in the context of long-maturity Treasury bonds. In general, Treasury bonds are actively traded right after they are issued, as a large part of them are initially bought not by their ultimate investors but by dealers and speculators. However, once a new Treasury of the same maturity is issued – which may be a month or two later, the now older security goes "off-the-run," as most trading interest shifts to the newly issued security and much of the old security's units are already included in portfolios of their ultimate investors who are less likely to trade them before maturity. Off-the-run securities are almost always less liquid than on-the-run securities of the same class, and this difference may be exploited to study whether and how illiquidity differences translate into a yield difference.

Warga (1992) studies holding period returns on constant duration portfolios of U.S. Treasury notes and bonds, and measures the yield premium generated by liquidity differences in bonds. He constructs portfolios of off-the-run and on-the-run bonds using durations within narrow ranges over the sample period 10/1982–12/1988, and finds a

---
[21] The inventory effect is consistent with the optimal dealer pricing policies derived by Amihud and Mendelson (1980).

consistent, positive and significant yield differential between them of 55 basis points per annum.

Krishnamurthi (2002) studies the price difference between the on-the-run and the most recent off-the-run 30-year bond. The price difference follows a systematic pattern over the auction cycle: It is highest right after the auction date and it declines to a small spread by the following auction date. To test whether the old bond–new bond yield difference results from a demand for liquid assets, Krishnamurthy regresses it on the yield spread between commercial paper and Treasury bills (both for three months), which represent demand for liquidity since commercial paper is less liquid than bills. Studying all 30-year bond auctions in the 1990s, he finds that the yield difference increases when the yield spread between commercial paper and bills increases, and that the relation is stronger far from an auction date, when the liquidity demand is strongest.

Further, Treasury bonds are often "on special" in the repo market which means that an owner can earn a "lending fee" by lending his bond to a short seller who must pay this fee. Krishnamurthy finds that new Treasury bonds are more special than old bonds. Hence, owners of new Treasury bonds can earn larger lending fees, which provides a partial explaination for why new bonds are more expensive (i.e. have lower yields). The differences in pricing, liquidity, and repo specialness between new and old bonds are consistent with the theories of Duffie et al. (2002) and Vayanos and Weill (2005) as described in Section 2.8.3.

Goldreich et al. (2003) study the varying value of liquidity over time, analyzing the liquidity and yields of two-year U.S. Treasury notes, comparing the very liquid on-the-run note with the most recent off-the-run note over the entire on/off-the-run cycle between the issue of the bond and the issue of the next bond. While the note is very liquid after issue and its buyer can expect to sell it to another buyer who will pay a premium for its liquidity, a buyer towards the end of the cycle may expect to sell the note when it goes off-the-run and becomes less liquid. Correspondingly, the yield difference between the off-the-run and the on-the-run notes decreases during the on-the-run cycle and approaches zero by the end of the cycle. Thus, the yield difference is driven by differences in expected *future* liquidity, rather than contemporaneous liquidity, where future liquidity is estimated by the average liquidity over the remainder of the cycle.

Goldreich et al. use GovPX data for 1/1994–12/2000, resulting in 56 two-year notes that were issued and matured through the period. The average yield difference between the on-the-run and off-the-run notes (adjusting for differences in the coupon rate and the yield curve) is about 1.5 basis point at the beginning of the cycle and it declines to zero by the end of the month. The liquidity variables that they consider are the quoted and effective bid–ask spread, the quote and trade size, the number of quotes and trades per day and the daily trading volume. The contemporaneous value of each such variable, denoted C, is C_t, and the expected future value is $\bar{C}_t = (C_{t+1} + C_{t+2} + \cdots + C_T)/(T - (t+1))$, obtained by averaging the future values of the variable over the remaining life of the security ($t = t+1, t+2, \ldots, T$). Goldreich et al. find that the difference in future liquidity, $\bar{C}_{off,t} - \bar{C}_{on,t}$, has strong explanatory power for the yield differential. When they consider both the contemporaneous and future liquidity variables jointly, future liquidity dominates. Finally, they find that the best explanatory liquidity variables are the quoted bid–ask spread and the quoted depth.

In Japan, an old government bond issue is effectively made to be on-the-run by designating it as the benchmark bond. It usually has a coupon similar to the coupon rate on newly-issued bonds and has large size, and following the designation, the benchmark bond becomes very liquid. Boudoukh and Whitelaw (1991) find that the yield on benchmark bonds is lower by about 30 to 100 basis points than the yield on bond issues with similar maturities and coupons, suggesting a sizable liquidity premium, especially in light of the fact that the average maturity of the benchmark bonds was 9.7 years over their study period.

Elton and Green (1998) examine the effect of liquidity on Treasury securities, where liquidity is measured by the trading volume in the interdealer market, obtained from the GovPX database for the period 1/1991–9/1995. Controlling for the tax type of the securities, they find significant differences between similar-maturity bonds that differ in their trading volumes. The difference between the price of a low-volume bond and the weighted average of a pair of high-volume bond with the same maturity but different coupons is negative and highly significant, meaning that the low-volume bond is cheaper and has a higher yield to maturity. However, their estimated price differential due to the liquidity difference for a sample of new bonds is small, 5 cents per $100 face value, and it is smaller for a sample of old bonds. In another test of the liquidity effect, Elton and Green fit a cubic spline price model to the after tax term structure, using the variable log(volume) to represent the bond's liquidity. The coefficient of this term is mostly positive, implying a higher price for more liquid bonds. The liquidity effect is small, though, amounting to 2.25 basis points, and it has been declining over the sample period. Notably, even after controlling for the liquidity effect (using the volume variable), there is a positive and significant price deviation for on-the-run bonds, perhaps reflecting an aspect of liquidity of these bonds not captured by volume such as repo specialness.

Longstaff (2004) provides another test of the effect of liquidity on bond yields by comparing yields on U.S. Treasury bonds with those on bonds issued by the Resolution Funding Corporation (Refcorp), a government agency. These bonds are effectively guaranteed by the U.S. Treasury and have the same default-free status as Treasury bonds. The difference between these bonds and Treasuries is in their liquidity: Refcorp bonds are less liquid than U.S. Treasury bonds. Longstaff compares the yield differential between zero-coupon Treasury and Refcorp bonds and finds that the average yield premium on Refcorp bonds ranges from 10 to 16 basis points, the differences being statistically significant (period: 4/1991–3/2001). This is a large liquidity premium which, for longer-term bonds, can represent 10%–15% of the value of the Treasury bond. There are considerable variations over time in this liquidity premium. Longstaff finds that it is negatively related to consumer confidence and to the change in the BBB–AAA credit spread, and positively related to Treasury buybacks. This means that the liquidity premium reacts to varying market conditions.

3.3.2 Corporate bonds

It has been suggested that the yield spread on corporate bonds – the yield in excess of the yield on Treasury bonds of the same maturity – is "too high" to be explained by default risk alone (Elton et al., 2001; Huang and Huang, 2003). Given that corporate bonds are generally less liquid than Treasury bonds, it stands to reason that the yield spread reflects in part a compensation for illiquidity. In analyzing corporate bonds, there is a problem of separating the risk premium from the illiquidity premium. Low-rated corporate bonds typically have both greater risk and lower liquidity, as is the case for stocks of risky and small companies. The results on the effects of liquidity depend, then, on the quality of the model that controls for the bond's risk.

Fisher (1959) studies the determinants of corporate bond "risk premium" – the yield spread – in cross-sectional regressions for the years 1927, 1932, 1937, 1949 and 1953. The determinants of the yield spread are default risk – proxied by the coefficient of variation of the firm's earnings, the period of solvency (the time it has been operating without a default) and its debt/equity ratio – and marketability, proxied by the market value of the firm's outstanding publicly-traded bonds (for lack of data on volume and bid–ask spreads). He finds a negative relationship between the logarithm of the risk premium and the marketability variable, as well as the expected signs for the variables proxying for default risk. These results mean that corporate bond yields reflect both risk and liquidity premiums.

The effect of liquidity on bond yields, using explicit measures for the cost of illiquidity, is studied by Chen et al. (2005). They measure illiquidity in three ways. One is the bound around the bond price within which new information would not trigger a transaction, estimated from daily data by the limited dependent variable model of Lesmond et al. (1999) (see Section 3.2.2 above), where the information variables are the daily change in the ten-year risk-free interest rate and the daily change in the S&P 500 index, both scaled by the bond's duration. The two other measures of illiquidity are the quoted bid–ask spread and the percent of zero spread and the percent of zero returns for a given year. The study examines a few thousand U.S. corporate bonds between 1995 and 2003 (the estimations use varying numbers of observations, depending on data availability). As may be expected, lower-rated bonds are more illiquid. Chen et al. then estimate a cross-sectional model of the corporate yield spread as a function of the three illiquidity variables as well as a number of variables that control for the bond's risk and its characteristics as well as the issuing firm's characteristics. The results show a significant positive effect of illiquidity on the yield spread, after controlling for the other variables (bond characteristics). The liquidity effect holds for both investment grade and speculative grade bonds, with the coefficient being larger for speculative-grade bonds. For example, in one estimate the authors divide the bonds in each category into three groups by their liquidity cost. They find that moving from one liquidity cost to a lower liquidity cost increases the yield spread by 37 basis points for investment-grade bonds and 128 basis points for speculative-grade bonds. The study further finds in a cross-section regression that annual *changes* in the bonds' yield spread are an increasing function of changes in the bond's illiquidity variables for both investment grade and speculative grade bonds (again, the regression controls for the changes in all other variables that reflect the bond and firm characteristics as well as macroeconomic factors). In conclusion, this study shows in a comprehensive way that the yield spread on corporate bonds reflects compensation for illiquidity as well as for risk.

The effect of liquidity *risk* on corporate bond yields is studied by De Jong and Driessen (2005), following Pastor and Stambaugh (2003) and Acharya and Pedersen (2005) (see section 3.2.4 above), using data from the U.S. and Europe (1/1993–2/2003). They employ a two-step multifactor procedure using two market risk factors, the equity market index return and the change in the implied volatility of equity index options, and two liquidity risk factors: Amihud (2002) illiquidity measure for equity, *ILLIQ*, and quoted bid–ask spreads on long-maturity U.S. Treasury bonds. In the first step they estimate the factor loadings and the liquidity betas of bond portfolios, aggregated by credit rating and maturity, by regressing the excess bond returns (over appropriate government bonds) on the market factors and the liquidity factor. The liquidity beta here is similar to the liquidity exposure coefficient in Pastor and Stambaugh (2003) and to β^{L2} in Acharya and Pedersen (2005). They find that lower-rated and longer-maturity bonds have greater exposure to the two indices of liquidity as well as greater exposure to the equity and risk factors. In the second step, they estimate whether the liquidity betas are priced by estimating a cross-section regression of the expected bond returns on the liquidity betas obtained from the first step, pegging the equity risk premium at some reasonable level. The two resulting liquidity exposures for their U.S. bond portfolios are highly correlated, but both are priced in the returns on corporate bonds. That is, corporate bonds with a higher exposure to stock and bond market illiquidity have higher expected returns. For the U.S. market, the total estimated liquidity premium is around 45 basis points for long-maturity investment grade bonds. For speculative grade bonds, which have higher exposures to the liquidity factors, the liquidity premium is around 100 basis points. The results for a sample of European corporate bonds are similar in spirit but insignificant in the cross-section analysis, perhaps due to small sample limitations (there are only 7 bond portfolios).

3.3.3 Rule 144A bonds

Some corporate bonds are traded in restricted markets. Rule 144A, approved by the Securities and Exchange Commission (SEC) on April 1990, allows firms to raise capital from "Qualified Institutional Buyers" (QIBs) without requiring registration of the securities and compliance with U.S. disclosure rules. The rule thus restricts trading in these securities to a purely-institutional market. Most of the securities issued under Rule 144A are corporate bonds. If liquidity affect asset prices, the yield spread (relative to Treasuries) on bonds that trade on Rule 144A markets should be higher than on bonds that trade on public markets. This is because public markets are more transparent and subject to disclosure rules that reduce informational asymmetries and increase liquidity.

Chaplinsky and Ramchand (2004) study the impact of Rule 144A on the cost of debt for international firms (1991–1997). They find, in a pooled cross-section regression of the yield spread on the Rule 144A dummy variable, as well as bond characteristics as controls, that Rule 144A bonds require a yield premium of 49 basis points on average. This pattern holds particularly for investment grade bonds.

Fenn (2000) too examines the difference between the yield spreads on bonds traded in the private and public markets. He posits that the yield differential declines over time, thus adding in his model an interaction variable, the product of a Rule 144A dummy variable and a time trend. He finds that the coefficient on the Rule 144A dummy variable is positive and significant (33 to 41 basis points, depending on specification), but the interaction variable is negative and significant (−8 basis points a year). However, Livingston and Zhou (2002), who study a later time period, find that the yield premium is strong and persistent, and Fenn's results are not robust to model specification. Livingston and Zhou estimate the yield differential between Rule 144A bonds and publicly-traded bonds, controlling for a number of variables: the first time the firm issued debt, the (log of) its issuing frequency, bond ratings, maturity, call protection, the default risk premium and indicators for senior debt and utility firms. They obtain that Rule 144A bonds have a higher yield, and dividing the sample by credit rating they obtain a yield differential of 35 basis points for the high-yield sample and 14 basis points for the investment grade sample. This is consistent with the notion that moving from the private to the public markets is a bigger step for high-yield than for investment-grade bonds, which is consequently worth more.

One may wonder why firms choose to issue less liquid debt under Rule 144A and incur the associated illiquidity cost. Fenn (2000) concludes that Rule 144A serves as a quick and convenient vehicle en route to issuing public securities: Rather than incur the delay of registering the securities with the SEC, firms sell them first to sophisticated investors who do not require registration, and after collecting the proceeds, they get to work at their leisure on registering the securities so they can be publicly traded.

3.4 Other financial instruments

In addition to stocks and bonds, liquidity affects the expected returns on other financial assets. In what follows, we discuss the effect of liquidity illiquid options, index-linked bonds, American Depository Receipts, hedge funds and closed-end funds. In each case, the price or expected return of the asset under study is compared to a benchmark asset with

3.4.1 Illiquid options

The effect of liquidity on option prices is unclear. The buyer and the seller may each demand a liquidity premium, but since the option value sums to zero between the two parties, it is unclear that the equilibrium price would reflect any liquidity premium. However, if the seller (writer) of the option does not demand a liquidity premium, the equilibrium price may reflect the liquidity premium demanded by the buyer. In Israel, the Bank of Israel issues European call options on the U.S. dollar paid in NIS (the Israeli currency), which are non-negotiable. Brenner et al. (2001) compare these options to ordinary options traded on the Tel Aviv Stock Exchange that are similar in their payoff but differ in their liquidity, the latter being far more liquid than the former. Brenner et al. compare the prices of three- and six-month at-the-money-forward options auctioned by the Bank of Israel, which are illiquid, to the same-day prices of synthetic publicly-traded options with a similar strike price and expiration date that they generate using the liquid options (period: 4/1994–6/1997, 272 and 127 options of 3 and 6 months, respectively). Because of the limited number of strike prices and expiration dates, it is impossible to exactly replicate the illiquid Bank of Israel option, and emulating its performance using publicly-traded option contracts entails transaction costs that total about 12%. They propose that the price (option premium) of the (synthetic) liquid option should be higher than the price of the illiquid option issued by the Bank of Israel. They find that the illiquid Bank of Israel option trades at a mean discount of 18% to 21% to the liquid (synthetic) option, highly significant.[22] The results are virtually unchanged when the estimation is performed separately for three- and six-month options. As the transaction costs to replicate the position have declined so did, later in time, the liquidity premium.

---
[22] There is a range of discounts because they use three different methods to create the synthetic option.

Empirical asset-pricing puzzles related to options are that index options are "expensive" (i.e. have high implied volatility relative to actual volatility), especially out-of-the-money put options, and that individual stock options are priced differently (i.e., are inexpensive and have less steep smile curves). Garleanu et al. (2004) address these puzzles using a model of demand pressure in which market makers can only hedge imperfectly. They show empirically that "end users" of options are net long index options, especially out-of-the-money puts, and net short individual stock options, and – employing the model – these demand pressures can help explain the option pricing puzzles. Equivalently, market makers are net short index volatility and net long individual stock options, and they want to be compensated for the risks associated with these positions, which helps explain the puzzles. Also, Bollen and Whaley (2004) show that signed order flow in options markets is related to changes in implied volatility, again reflecting market makers' inability to perfectly absorb demand pressures, and discuss the option-pricing implications.

3.4.2 Index-linked bonds

Dimson and Hanke (2002) test the existence of a liquidity effect by comparing instruments with similar cash flows that differ only in their liquidity. They analyze equity index-linked bonds which provide the same payoff as an investment in an equity index[23] but have finite (typically 10–15 year) maturities and their trading volume and transaction frequencies are low, i.e., they have low liquidity. Because they are issued in small quantities and are immediately repayable if the asset cover drops below a pre-specified level, their default risk is very low. Dimson and Hanke use transaction data for all equity index-linked bonds traded on the London Stock Exchange for their entire history (through 2001). They find that the prices of these bonds is discounted by an average of 2.71% relative to their underlying value, with the discount being an

---

[23] Equity-linked index bonds have a principal that is linked to an equity market index and a coupon that equals the dividend yield of the underlying equity index. At maturity, investors receive a payment equal to the level of the index.

76 *Empirical Evidence*

increasing function of bonds' bid–ask spread. Using the time series of the discounts, discounts, they show that liquidity risk has a systematic component, and relate this market-wide factor to a number of macroeconomic variables that have previously been shown to be related (at least partially) to illiquidity: The small-firm premium and the changes in closed-end fund discounts, the bond maturity premium, U.S. stock market turnover, credit spread over Treasuries and futures basis for the FTSE 100 contract.

3.4.3 American depository receipts (ADRs)

ADRs (American Depository Receipts) enable to compare two identical securities with the same payoffs but with different liquidity. ADRs are negotiable certificates of ownership of shares for foreign securities which may be listed on a U.S. stock market. They entitle the holders to the same cash flows as does the underlying stock in the foreign country but due to the difference in their trading venue, there may be a difference between the liquidity of the ADR and of its underlying stock.

Chan et al. (2005a) study 401 pairs of ADRs and underlying stocks, relating the price difference between them to differences in their liquidity.[24] The study uses ADRs that were listed on the New York Stock Exchange, the American Stock Exchange or the NASDAQ stock market from 23 countries for the period 1981–2003.[25] They propose that the ADR premium – the price differential relative to the underlying stock's price (all converted to U.S. dollars) – is an increasing function of the ADR liquidity in the U.S. market and a declining function of the liquidity of the underlying stock and of the liquidity of the market in the foreign country. The study employs three liquidity measures: (i) Amihud (2002) *ILLIQ* (see Section 3.2.1 above), (ii) the security's turnover (the ratio of volume to shares outstanding), and (iii) the trading infrequency (the percentage of days on which the security did not trade

---

[24] See also Rabinovitch et al. (2003) on the relationship between ADR liquidity and returns on ADRs versus the return on the underlying stocks.

[25] Foerster and Karolyi (1999) show that foreign firms that cross-list their shares as ADRs earn on average cumulative abnormal returns of 19% during the year before listing, and an additional 1.2% during the listing week, of which they lose 14% in the year following listing. They focus, however, on Merton (1987) investor recognition hypothesis.

over the month). The measures are calculated for each ADR for each month, and the first two measures are also calculated for the underlying stock and for the home country by averaging each over the stocks from each country (trading frequency did not vary for the underlying stocks in their home country because these stocks were frequently traded).

Chan et al. (2005a) estimate cross-sectional monthly regressions of the ADR premium over the different liquidity measures, and calculate the coefficients by the Fama and MacBeth (1973) method. The results support the hypothesis of a positive price–liquidity relationship. The coefficients of the ADR premium on ADR liquidity (illiquidity) are positive (negative) and significant for all three measures. The coefficient of the underlying stock's *ILLIQ* is positive and significant, and that of the underlying stock's turnover is negative and significant – again, consistent with the hypothesis that liquidity is priced. These results are robust and continue to hold with controls for the ADR size, 1- and 6-month home stock market return, and 1- and 6-month exchange rate returns. The home country's *ILLIQ* has the expected sign but with lower explanatory power, and it is statistically insignificant in some models. In summary, the liquidity of the ADR vis-à-vis the underlying stock appears to be an important driver of the ADR premium. The effect of the ADR's illiquidity on its premium continue to hold in a cross-sectional regression of the monthly *changes* in these variables, particularly for the turnover and trading frequency measures; changes in the underlying stock's liquidity, as well as in the home country's liquidity, are insignificant.

3.4.4 Hedge funds

Hedge funds are private investment partnerships which can follow flexible investment strategies, take both long and short positions, use leverage and derivatives and invest in a variety of assets and markets. Liang (1999) studies how hedge fund characteristics affect their returns using a sample of 385 hedge funds that reported monthly returns over the 1/1994–12/1996 period. One of his explanatory variables is the fund lockup period, the number of days since the initial investment the investor's shares are "locked up" and cannot be redeemed, which constrains the investors' liquidity (other fund characteristics included in his regressions are the fund's incentive fee, management fee, log(assets) and age since the fund's inception). While most funds in the sample did not have a lockup period, the mean lockup period across all funds (including the zeros) was 84 days, with a standard deviation of 164 days.[26] The results show that the coefficient of monthly return on the lockup period is positive and significant, consistent with a positive liquidity premium. Liang concludes that "the lockup period is critical in determining fund returns" (p. 78).

In a comprehensive analysis of the effects of liquidity on hedge fund returns, Aragon (2004) studies the relationship between the liquidation restrictions on hedge funds and their returns. The study considers two liquidity variables: (i) the lockup provision, indicated by a lockup dummy (the lockup period is usually the same, around one year), which applies to 18% of the funds, and (ii) the fund's redemption notice period, which is the number of days investors are required to give advance notice before redeeming their shares. The redemption period averages 26 days across the entire sample (28% of sample funds do not have an advance notice requirement). The study uses monthly data from the TASS Tremont database for 2,871 hedge funds over the period 1/1994–12/2001.

Aragon finds that the annual return on a portfolio of funds with lockup provisions is higher than the return on a portfolio of funds without such provision (within a multifactor model). The difference is 7%–8% for equally-weighted portfolios and 4%–5% for value-weighted portfolios.[27] In a pooled time-series and cross-section factor model of the monthly returns as a function of the lockup dummy and the notice period as well as the minimum investment size, the coefficients of both liquidity variables are positive and significant. The coefficient of the lockup dummy is 6.2%–7.6%, and the excess annual return associated

---

[26] The lockup periods for funds that have them are generally around a year. Liang (1999) statistics are consistent with about a quarter of the funds having a lockup period around one year, and about three quarters of the funds having no lockup period.

[27] Aragon (2004) explains the return difference between equally-weighted and value-weighted portfolios by the dependence on fund age.

with the notice period is about 2% per month of advance notice. After controlling for these variables, the constant coefficients are not statistically different from zero. That is, the excess returns on hedge funds may be fully attributable to the special liquidation restrictions that they impose. As a further test of the theory, Aragon (2004) estimates the pooled regression with quadratic forms for the notice period and minimum investment variables. Because of the clientele effect discussed in Section 2.3, expected return should be a concave function of illiquidity, suggesting a negative coefficient of the squared illiquidity variables. The results show that the coefficients on the squared illiquidity variables are indeed negative and significant, again confirming the theoretical predictions.[28]

3.4.5 Closed-end funds

Closed-end funds, unlike their open-end counterparts, have a fixed number of shares, they trade like ordinary stocks and are priced in the market. Funds that hold domestic securities typically trade at a discount to their net asset value, or a negative premium, where the premium is the excess value of the fund's price over its NAV (net asset value). The negative premium is typically explained by investor sentiment and other behavioral factors, or by a capitalization of the management fee. Another explanation is the difference between the liquidity of closed-end funds and that of their underlying securities. Then, liquidity differences across funds between the liquidity of the fund's stock and the liquidity of the stocks in its portfolio may explain differences in fund premiums.

Datar (2001) studies the impact of market liquidity on the premium (= fund's price/NAV $-$ 1) on closed-end funds, based on the relationship between the liquidity of the fund's shares and the liquidity of the assets held in the fund's portfolio. He tests the hypothesis that within a group of funds that hold similar assets (stocks or bonds), the closed-end fund premium increases as the liquidity of the funds' shares increases.

---

[28] Aragon obtains similar results when he uses a two-pass approach which first estimates the multifactor model for each fund separately, and then uses a cross sectional regression with the fund's α as the dependent variable and the above variables as independent variables.

Using weekly data for closed-end funds listed on the NYSE, Datar tests this hypothesis and indeed finds the expected positive relationship between the fund premium and the liquidity of the funds' shares. As liquidity measures, Datar uses (the logarithms of) the funds' share and dollar trading volumes, shares outstanding and fund size, turnover and volatility. Using a number of alternative specifications, he shows the results are robust. The results thus support the liquidity explanation for the closed-end fund discount.

Manzler (2004) shows that the discounts on closed-end funds are driven by both liquidity and liquidity risk differentials between the fund stocks and the stocks in the underlying portfolio. First, he calculates the portfolio liquidity – the value-weighted average of the liquidity of its component stocks – and the liquidity of the fund's shares using two measures, a modified *ILLIQ* measure and the quoted bid–ask spread. The study spans the 1995–2003 period, where data on the portfolios of 37 funds were compiled from quarterly reports. Manzler finds that the closed-end fund premium increases (or its discount decreases) in the difference between the illiquidity on the fund's portfolio and the illiquidity of the fund's shares (the results are significant only when using *ILLIQ*).

Next, Manzler proposes that as the liquidity *risk* of closed-end funds increases relative to the liquidity risk of their portfolios, the fund premium should be lower (or the discount greater). To that end, he constructs an illiquidity factor, the return series on illiquid-minus-liquid (IML) stocks, obtained by ranking stocks into deciles by the magnitude of the residuals from an AR(2) model of their *ILLIQ* measure and then taking the difference between the returns on the extreme portfolios. He then regresses the returns on the funds and their NAV on a three-factor Fama–French model that has an additional illiquidity factor, IML. Finally, the average three-year premia are regressed across funds on the differences between the fund betas and the underlying portfolio betas. Focusing on the IML betas, the results are that the fund premium declines in the difference between the fund's illiquidity beta and the illiquidity beta of its portfolio. That is, the higher the liquidity risk of a closed-end fund relative to its underlying portfolio, the larger the closed-end fund discount.

Cherkes et al. (2005) develop a liquidity-based model of closed-end funds that shows they provide investors a way to buy illiquid securities at lower illiquidity costs. Their model predicts that closed-end fund IPOs take place in waves, a sector at a time, with the fund share initially issued at a premium to net asset value that often turns later into a discount. They show, using Morningstar data over the 1986–2004 period, that the behavior of closed-end fund premiums generally conforms with the predictions of their model. Empirically, they find that in a time series regression of the closed-end fund premium on the Pastor and Stambaugh (2003) liquidity measure, the coefficient is negative, suggesting that closed-end funds are more valuable when market liquidity worsens.

Liquidity differences are accentuated for closed-end country funds which issue shares in the U.S. and invest the proceeds in the shares of companies in a foreign country or region. Unlike domestic funds, country funds tend to have positive fund premiums which vary substantially over time and across countries. Similar to the case of ADRs, closed-end country funds enable to test the liquidity effect, in this case – the relationship between liquidity differences and fund premiums. This task is undertaken by Chan et al. (2005b), who study a sample of 41 single-country closed end funds from 29 different countries that traded in the U.S. over the 8/1987–12/2001 period. The hypothesis is that if the home and U.S. market are segmented, lower home market liquidity should decrease only the NAV, which will increase the fund premium, whereas lower liquidity in the U.S. market should reduce only the fund's price, thereby decreasing the fund premium. In an integrated market, however, where liquidity shocks in one market spill over to the other market, the prices of the fund and its underlying assets should converge. The study distinguishes between segmented and integrated markets using the Edison and Warnock (2003) measure of capital control. In all, 16 funds are in integrated markets and 26 funds in segmented markets. The illiquidity of a country's market is calculated using Amihud (2002) *ILLIQ* measure: A country *ILLIQ* is an equally-weighted average of the illiquidity of all qualifying individual stocks in the representative market index for that market (which is usually quite broad-based). The illiquidity measure is calculated every month (values are in logs).

Chan et al. (2005b) first estimate a pooled model with fixed fund effects where the fund premium is a function of the illiquidity of the U.S. market and the illiquidity of the foreign market as key explanatory variables, in addition to control variables (capital controls, the fund's expense ratio, size, dividend yield, fund age, degree of institutional ownership, market returns in the U.S. and in the home market and the foreign exchange appreciation rate). A monthly time-series control variable is the average premium of all funds, thus capturing any investor sentiment effect. The results are consistent with the hypothesis for the segmented markets: The fund premium declines in the U.S. market's illiquidity and increases in the foreign market's illiquidity, with the coefficients being statistically significant. For the integrated market, the effect is reversed although the significance of the coefficients is not robust to model specification.

Next, a cross-sectional test regresses the monthly fund premiums on the explanatory variables, employing the Fama and MacBeth (1973) method. Since the illiquidity of the U.S. market is constant across all funds in every month, the study uses instead the exposure of the fund's premium to the U.S. market's illiquidity, consistent with Pastor and Stambaugh (2003) γ and with Acharya and Pedersen (2005) β^{L2}. This is obtained as the beta coefficient from a regression of the fund's premium on the U.S. illiquidity. (Also, the U.S. market return is replaced by the beta coefficient of the fund's return on the U.S. market return.) The U.S. liquidity beta, which is negative, has a negative and significant coefficient, implying that the liquidity risk is priced in the fund's premium. The coefficient is larger and significant for the integrated markets funds and is insignificant for the segmented markets funds. Country illiquidity has a positive and statistically significant coefficient for the segmented markets funds, and it is insignificantly different from zero for the integrated markets funds. In sum, Chan et al. (2005b) conclude that the premiums on closed-end country funds are largely explained by illiquidity considerations: Their empirical results show that market illiquidity accounts for 35% of the time-series and 12% of the cross-sectional variation in fund premiums.

References

Acharya, V. V. and L. H. Pedersen (2005), 'Asset pricing with liquidity risk'. *Journal of Financial Economics* **77**, 375–410.

Admati, A. R. and P. Pfleiderer (1988), 'A theory of intraday patterns: Volume and price variability'. *Review of Financial Studies* **1**, 3–40.

Admati, A. R. (1985), 'A noisy rational expectations equilibrium for multi-asset securities markets'. *Econometrica* **53**, 629–657.

Akerlof, G. A. (1970), 'The market for lemons: Quality uncertainty and the market mechanism'. *Quarterly Journal of Economics* **84**, 488–500.

Allen, F. and D. Gale (2004), 'Financial intermediaries and markets'. *Econometrica* **72**, 1023–1061.

Allen, F. and D. Gale (2005), 'Financial fragility, liquidity, and asset prices'. *Journal of the European Economic Association* **2**, 1015–1048.

Amihud, Y., B. Lauterbach, and H. Mendelson (2003), 'The value of trading consolidation: Evidence from the exercise of warrants'. *Journal of Financial and Quantitative Analysis* **38**, 829–846.

Amihud, Y., H. Mendelson, and B. Lauterbach (1997), 'Market microstructure and securities values: Evidence from the Tel Aviv Exchange'. *Journal of Financial Economics* **45**, 365–390.

References

Amihud, Y., H. Mendelson, and J. Uno (1999), 'Number of shareholders and stock prices: Evidence from Japan'. *Journal of Finance* **54**, 1169–1184.

Amihud, Y., H. Mendelson, and R. Wood (1990), 'Liquidity and the 1987 stock market crash'. *Journal of Portfolio Management* **16**, 65–69.

Amihud, Y. and H. Mendelson (1980), 'Dealership markets: Market making with inventory'. *Journal of Financial Economics* **8**, 21–53.

Amihud, Y. and H. Mendelson (1986a), 'Asset pricing and the bid-ask spread'. *Journal of Financial Economics* **17**, 223–249.

Amihud, Y. and H. Mendelson (1986b), 'Liquidity and stock returns'. *Financial Analysts Journal* **42**, 43–48.

Amihud, Y. and H. Mendelson (1987), 'Trading mechanisms and stock returns: An empirical investigation'. *Journal of Finance* **42**, 533–553.

Amihud, Y. and H. Mendelson (1989), 'The effects of beta, bid-ask spread, residual risk and size on stock returns'. *Journal of Finance* **44**, 479–486.

Amihud, Y. and H. Mendelson (1991a), 'Liquidity, maturity and the yields on U.S. government securities'. *Journal of Finance* **46**, 1411–1426.

Amihud, Y. and H. Mendelson (1991b), 'Liquidity, asset prices and financial policy'. *Financial Analysts Journal* **47**, 56–66.

Amihud, Y. and H. Mendelson (1991), 'Liquidity, maturity, and the yields on U.S. Treasury securities'. *Journal of Finance* **46**, 1411–1425.

Amihud, Y. (2002), 'Illiquidity and stock returns: Cross-section and time series effects'. *Journal of Financial Markets* **5**, 31–56.

Angel, J. J., J. H. Harris, V. Panchapagesan, and I. M. Werner (2005), 'From pink slips to pink sheets: Liquidity and shareholder wealth consequences of Nasdaq delistings'. Working Paper, Ohio State University.

Aragon, G. O. (2004), 'Share restrictions and asset pricing: Evidence from the hedge fund industry'. Working Paper, Boston College.

Atkins, A. B. and E. A. Dyl (1997), 'Transactions costs and holding periods for common stocks'. *Journal of Finance* **52**, 309–325.

Attari, M., A. S. Mello, and M. E. Ruckes (2005), 'Arbitraging arbitrageurs'. *Journal of Finance*. Forthcoming.

Bagehot, W. P. (1971), 'The only game in town'. *Financial Analysts Journal* **22**, 12–14.

Balduzzi, P. and A. Lynch (1999), 'Transaction costs and predictability: Some utility cost calculations'. *Journal of Financial Economics* **52**, 47–78.

Banz, R. W. (1981), 'The relationship between return and market value of common stocks'. *Journal of Financial Economics* **9**, 3–18.

Bekaert, G., C. R. Harvey, and C. Lundblad (2005), 'Liquidity and expected returns: Lessons from emerging markets'. Working Paper, Columbia University.

Benston, G. and R. Hagerman (1974), 'Determinants of the bid-ask spreads in the over-the-counter markets'. *Journal of Financial Economics* **1**, 353–364.

Berkman, H. and V. R. Eleswarapu (1998), 'Short-term traders and liquidity: A test using Bombay stock exchange data'. *Journal of Financial Economics* **47**, 339–355.

Biais, B., L. R. Glosten, and C. S. Spatt (2002), 'The microstructure of stock markets'. *Journal of Financial Intermediation*. Forthcoming.

Bollen, N. P. and R. E. Whaley (2004), 'Does net buying pressure affect the shape of implied volatility functions?'. *Journal of Finance* **59**, 711–753.

Boudoukh, J. and R. F. Whitelaw (1991), 'The benchmark effect in the Japanese government bond market'. *Journal of Fixed Income* **1/2**, 52–59.

Boudoukh, J. and R. F. Whitelaw (1993), 'Liquidity as a choice variable: A lesson from the Japanese government bond market'. *The Review of Financial Studies* **6**, 265–292.

Brennan, M. J., T. Chordia, and A. Subrahmanyam (1998), 'Alternative factor specifications, security characteristics, and the cross-section of expected stock returns'. *Journal of Financial Economics* **49**, 345–373.

Brennan, M. J. and A. Subrahmanyam (1996), 'Market microstructure and asset pricing: On the compensation for illiquidity in stock returns'. *Journal of Financial Economics* **41**, 441–464.

References

Brenner, M., R. Eldor, and S. Hauser (2001), 'The price of options illiquidity'. *Journal of Finance* **56**, 789–805.

Brunnermeier, M. and L. H. Pedersen (2005a), 'Market liquidity and funding liquidity'. Working Paper, Princeton University.

Brunnermeier, M. and L. H. Pedersen (2005b), 'Predatory trading'. *Journal of Finance* **60**, 1825–1863.

Campbell, J. Y., S. J. Grossman, and J. Wang (1993), 'Trading volume and serial correlation in stock returns'. *Quarterly Journal of Economics* **108**, 905–939.

Cao, H. H., M. D. Evans, and R. K. Lyons (2003), 'Inventory information'. Working Paper, University of North Carolina.

Chalmers, J. M. R. and G. B. Kadlec (1998), 'An empirical examination of the amortized spread'. *Journal of Financial Economics* **48**, 159–188.

Chan, J. S. P., D. Hong, and M. G. Subrahmanyam (2005a), 'Liquidity and asset prices in multiple markets'. Working Paper, NYU.

Chan, J. S. P., R. Jain, and Y. Xia (2005b), 'Market segmentation, liquidity spillover, and closed-end country fund discounts'. Working Paper, Singapore Management University.

Chaplinsky, S. and L. Ramchand (2004), 'The borrowing costs of international issuers: SEC Rule 144A'. *The Journal of Business* **77**, 1073–1097.

Chen, L., D. A. Lesmond, and J. Z. Wei (2005), 'Corporate yield spreads and bond liquidity'. *Journal of Finance*. Forthcoming.

Chen, Z. and P. Xiong (2001), 'Discounts on illiquid stocks: Evidence from China'. Working Paper, Yale University.

Cherkes, M., J. Sagi, and R. Stanton (2005), 'Liquidity and closed-end funds'. Working Paper, Princeton University.

Chordia, T., R. Roll, and A. Subrahmanyam (2002), 'Commonality in liquidity'. *Journal of Financial Economics* **56**, 3–28.

Chordia, T., A. Sarkar, and A. Subramaniam (2005), 'The joint dynamics of liquidity, returns, and volatility across small and large firms'. Working Paper, UCLA.

Chordia, T., A. Subrahmanyam, and V. R. Anshuman (2001), 'Trading activity and expected stock returns'. *Journal of Financial Economics* **59**, 3–32.

Cochrane, J. H. (2001), *Asset Pricing*. Princeton University Press, New Jersey.

Cochrane, J. H. (2005), 'Asset pricing program review: Liquidity, trading and asset prices'. NBER Reporter.

Connor, G. and R. Korajczyk (1988), 'Risk and return in an equilibrium apt: Application of a new test methodology'. *Journal of Financial Economics* **21**, 255–290.

Constantinides, G. M. (1986), 'Capital market equilibrium with transaction costs'. *Journal of Political Economy* **94**, 842–862.

Copeland, T. E. and D. Galai (1983), 'Informational effects on the bid ask spread'. *Journal of Finance* **38**, 1457–1469.

Datar, V. T., N. Y. Naik, and R. Radcliffe (1998), 'Liquidity and stock returns: An alternative test'. *Journal of Financial Markets* **1**, 205–219.

Datar, V. (2001), 'Impact of liquidity on premia/discounts in closed-end funds'. *The Quarterly Review of Economics and Finance* **41**, 119–135.

Davis, M. and A. Norman (1990), 'Portfolio selection with transaction costs'. *Mathematics of Operations Research* **15**, 676–713.

De Jong, F. and J. Driessen (2005), 'Liquidity risk premia in corporate bond markets'. Working Paper, University of Amsterdam.

Dimson, E. and B. Hanke (2002), 'The expected illiquidity premium: Evidence from equity index-linked bonds'. Working Paper.

Duffie, D., N. Garleanu, and L. H. Pedersen (2002), 'Securities lending, shorting, and pricing'. *Journal of Financial Economics* **66**, 307–339.

Duffie, D., N. Garleanu, and L. H. Pedersen (2003), 'Valuation in over the-counter markets'. Working Paper, Stanford University.

Duffie, D., N. Garleanu, and L. H. Pedersen (2005), 'Over-the-counter markets'. *Econometrica* **73**, 1815–1847.

Duffie, D. (1996), *Dynamic Asset Pricing Theory*. Princeton University Press, New Jersey, second edition.

Easley, D., S. Hvidkjaer, and M. O'Hara (2002), 'Is information risk a determinant of asset returns?'. *Journal of Finance* **57**, 2185–2221.

Easley, D., N. M. Kiefer, and M. O'Hara (1997), 'One day in the life of a very common stock'. *Review of Financial Studies* **10**, 805–835.

Easley, D. and M. O'Hara (1987), 'Price, trade size, and information in securities markets'. *Journal of Financial Economics* **19**, 69–90.

Easley, D. and M. O'Hara (2003), 'Microstructure and asset pricing'. In: G. Constantinides, M. Harris, and R. Stulz (eds.): *Handbook of Financial Economics*. B.V. North Holland, Elsevier Science Publishers.

Easley, D. and M. O'Hara (2004), 'Information and the cost of capital'. *Journal of Finance* **59**, 1553–1583.

Edison, H. J. and F. E. Warnock (2003), 'A simple measure of the intensity of capital controls'. *Journal of Empirical Finance* **10**, 81–103.

Eleswarapu, V. R. and M. Reinganum (1993), 'The seasonal behavior of liquidity premium in asset pricing'. *Journal of Financial Economics* **34**, 373–386.

Eleswarapu, V. R. (1997), 'Cost of transacting and expected returns in the Nasdaq market'. *Journal of Finance* **52**, 2113–2127.

Elton, E. J. and T. C. Green (1998), 'Tax and liquidity effects in pricing of government bonds'. *Journal of Finance* **53**, 1533–62.

Elton, E. J., M. J. Gruber, D. Agrawal, and C. Mann (2001), 'On the valuation of corporate bonds using rating-based models'. Working Paper, New York University.

Elyasiani, E., S. Hauser, and B. Lauterbach (2000), 'Market response to liquidity improvements: Evidence from exchange listing'. *Financial Review* **41**, 1–14.

Fama, E. F. and K. R. French (1992), 'The cross section of expected stock returns'. *Journal of Finance* **47**, 427–465.

Fama, E. F. and K. R. French (1993), 'Common risk factors in the returns on stocks and bonds'. *Journal of Financial Economics* **33**, 3–56.

Fama, E. F. and J. D. MacBeth (1973), 'Risk, return and equilibrium: Empirical tests'. *Journal of Political Economy* **81**, 607–636.

Fenn, G. W. (2000), 'Speed of issuance and the adequacy of disclosure in the 144A high-yield debt market'. *Journal of Financial Economics* **56**, 383–406.

Fisher, L. (1959), 'Determinants of risk premiums on corporate bonds'. *Journal of Political Economy* **xx**, 217–237.

Foerster, S. and G. A. Karolyi (1999), 'The effects of market segmentation and investor recognition on asset prices: Evidence of foreign stock listings in the U.S.'. *Journal of Finance* **54**, 981–1014.

Fujimoto, A. and M. Watanabe (2005), 'Time-varying liquidity risk and the cross-section of stock returns'. Working Paper, University of Alberta and Rice University.

Gallmeyer, M. F., B. Hollifield, and D. J. Seppi (2004), 'Liquidity discovery and asset pricing'. Working Paper, Carnegie Mellon University.

Garbade, K. D. and W. L. Silber (1979), 'Structural organization of secondary markets: Clearing frequency, dealer activity and liquidity risk'. *Journal of Finance* **34**, 577–593.

Garbade, K. D. (1984), 'Analyzing the structure of Treasury yields: Duration, coupon, and liquidity effects'. *Topics in Money and Securities Markets*. Bankers Trust Company.

Garleanu, N., L. H. Pedersen, and A. Poteshman (2004), 'Demand-based option pricing'. Working Paper, The Wharton School.

Garleanu, N. and L. H. Pedersen (2004), 'Adverse selection and the required return'. *Review of Financial Studies* **17**, 643–665.

Garman, M. B. (1976), 'Market microstructure'. *Journal of Financial Economics* **3**, 257–275.

Gelman, M. (1972), 'An economist-financial analyst's approach to valuing stock of a closely held company'. *Journal of Taxation* **xx**, 353.

Glosten, L. R. and L. Harris (1988), 'Estimating the components of the bid-ask spread'. *Journal of Financial Economics* **21**, 123–142.

Glosten, L. R. and P. R. Milgrom (1985), 'Bid, ask and transaction prices in a specialist market with heterogeneously informed traders'. *Journal of Financial Economics* **14**, 71–100.

Goldreich, D., B. Hanke, and P. Nath (2003), 'The price of future liquidity: Time-varying liquidity in the U.S. Treasury market'. Working Paper, London Business School.

Gottesman, A. and G. Jacoby (2005), 'Payout policy, taxes, and the relation between returns and the bid-ask spread'. *Journal of Banking and Finance*. Forthcoming.

Gromb, D. and D. Vayanos (2002), 'Equilibrium and welfare in markets with financially constraint arbitrageurs'. *Journal of Financial Economics* **66**, 361–407.

Grossman, S. J. and M. H. Miller (1988), 'Liquidity and market structure'. *Journal of Finance* **43**, 617–633.

Grossman, S. J. and J. E. Stiglitz (1980), 'On the impossibility of informationally efficient markets'. *American Economic Review* **70**, 393–408.

Grossman, S. J. (1976), 'On the efficiency of competitive stock markets where traders have diverse information'. *Journal of Finance* **31**, 573–585.

Harris, L. E. (2003), *Trading and Exchanges*. Oxford University Press, New York.

Hasbrouck, J. and D. Seppi (2001), 'Common factors in prices, order flows, and liquidity'. *Journal of Financial Economics* **59**, 383–411.

Hasbrouck, J. (1991), 'Measuring the information content of stock trades'. *Journal of Finance* **46**, 179–207.

Hasbrouck, J. (2005), 'Inferring trading costs from daily data: US equities for 1962 to 2001'. Working Paper, NYU Stern.

Heaton, J. and D. Lucas (1996), 'Evaluating the effects of incomplete markets on risk sharing and asset pricing'. *Journal of Political Economy* **104**, 443–487.

Hegde, S. P. and J. B. McDermott (2003), 'The liquidity effects of revisions to the S&P 500 index: An empirical analysis'. *Journal of Financial Markets* **6**, 413–459.

Hellwig, M. F. (1980), 'On the aggregation of information in competitive markets'. *Journal of Economic Theory* **22**, 477–498.

Holmström, B. and J. Tirole (1998), 'Private and public supply of liquidity'. *Journal of Political Economy* **106**, 1–39.

Holmström, B. and J. Tirole (2001), 'LAPM: A liquidity-based asset pricing model'. *Journal of Finance* **56**, 1837–1867.

Hopenhayn, H. A. and I. M. Werner (1996), 'Information, liquidity, and asset trading in a random matching game'. *Journal of Economic Theory* **68**, 349–379.

Ho, T. S. Y. and H. R. Stoll (1981), 'Optimal dealer pricing under transactions and return uncertainty'. *Journal of Financial Economics* **9**, 47–73.

Ho, T. S. Y. and H. R. Stoll (1983), 'The dynamics of dealer markets under competition'. *Journal of Finance* **38**, 1053–1074.

Huang, J. and M. Huang (2003), 'How much of the corporate-treasury yield spread is due to credit risk?'. Working Paper, Stanford University.

Huang, M. (2003), 'Liquidity shocks and equilibrium liquidity premia'. *Journal of Economic Theory* **109**, 104–129.

Huberman, G. and D. Halka (2001), 'Systematic liquidity'. *Journal of Financial Research* **24**, 161–178.

Hu, S.-Y. (1997), 'Trading turnover and expected stock returns: The trading frequency hypothesis and evidence from the Tokyo Stock Exchange'. Working Paper, National Taiwan University.

Jacoby, G., D. J. Fowler, and A. A. Gottesman (2000), 'The capital asset pricing model and the liquidity effect: A theoretical approach'. *Journal of Financial Markets* **3**, 69–81.

Jang, B.-G., H. K. Koo, H. Liu, and M. Loewenstein (2005), 'Liquidity premia and transactions costs'. Working Paper.

Jones, C. (2002), 'A century of stock market liquidity and trading costs'. Working Paper, Columbia University.

Kadlec, G. B. and J. J. McConnell (1994), 'The effect of market segmentation and illiquidity on asset prices: Evidence from exchange listings'. *Journal of Finance* **49**, 611–636.

Kalay, A., L. Wei, and A. Wohl (2002), 'Continuous trading or call auctions: Revealed preferences of investors at TASE'. *Journal of Finance* **57**, 523–542.

Kamara, A. (1994), 'Liquidity, taxes, and short-term treasury yields'. *Journal of Financial and Quantitative Analysis* **29**, 403–416.

Kane, A. (1994), 'The trading cost premium in capital asset returns – a closed form solution'. *Journal of Banking and Finance* **18**, 1177–1183.

Keim, D. (1983), 'Size-related anomalies and stock return seasonality'. *Journal of Financial Economics* **12**, 13–32.

Kraus, A. and H. R. Stoll (1972), 'Price impacts of block trading on the New York stock exchange'. *Journal of Finance* **27**, 569–588.

Krishnamurthi, A. (2002), 'The bond/old-bond spread'. *Journal of Financial Economics* **66**, 463–506.

Kyle, A. S. (1985), 'Continuous auctions and insider trading'. *Econometrica* **53**, 1315–1335.

Kyle, A. S. (1989), 'Informed speculation with imperfect competition'. *Review of Economic Studies* **56**, 317–355.

Lagos, R. (2005), 'Asset prices and liquidity in an exchange economy'. Working Paper, New York University.

Lamont, O. A. and R. H. Thaler (2003), 'Can the market add and subtract? Mispricing in tech stock carve-outs'. *Journal of Political Economy* **111**, 227–268.

Lauterbach, B. (2001), 'A note on trading mechanism and securities value: The analysis of rejects from continuous trade'. *Journal of Banking and Finance* **25**, 419–430.

Lesmond, D., J. Ogden, and C. Trzcinka (1999), 'A new estimate of transaction costs'. *Review of Financial Studies* **12**, 1113–1141.

Levy, H. (1978), 'Equilibrium in an imperfect market: A constraint on the number of securities in the portfolio'. *American Economic Review* **68**, 643–658.

Liang, B. (1999), 'On the performance of hedge funds'. *Financial Analysts Journal* **55**, 72–85.

Lintner, J. (1965), 'The valuation of risk assets and the selection of risky investments in stock portfolios and capital budgets'. *Review of Economics and Statistics* **47**, 13–37.

Litzenberger, R. H. and K. Ramaswamy (1979), 'The effect of personal taxes and dividends on capital asset prices: Theory and empirical evidence'. *Journal of Financial Economics* **7**, 163–195.

Liu, H. (2004a), 'Optimal consumption and investment with transaction costs and multiple assets'. *Journal of Finance* **59**, 289–338.

Liu, W. (2004b), 'Liquidity premium and a two-factor model'. Working Paper, University of Manchester, Manchester School of Accounting and Finance.

Livingston, M. and L. Zhou (2002), 'The impact of Rule 144A debt offerings upon bond yields and underwriter fees'. *Financial Management* **xx**, 5–27.

Loderer, C. and L. Roth (2005), 'The pricing discount for limited liquidity: Evidence from SWX Swiss Exchange and the Nasdaq'. *Journal of Empirical Finance* **12**, 239–268.

Longstaff, F. A. (2001), 'Optimal portfolio choice and the valuation of illiquid securities'. *Review of Financial Studies* **14**, 407–431.

Longstaff, F. A. (2004), 'The flight-to-liquidity premium in U.S. Treasury bond prices'. *Journal of Business*. Forthcoming.

Longstaff, F. (1995), 'How much can marketability affect security values?'. *The Journal of Finance* **50**, 1767–1774.

Lo, A. W., H. Mamaysky, and J. Wang (2004), 'Asset prices and trading volume under fixed transaction costs'. *Journal of Political Economy* **112**, 1054–1090.

Luttmer, E. G. (1996), 'Asset pricing in economies with frictions'. *Econometrica* **64**, 1439–1467.

Luttmer, E. G. (1999), 'What level of fixed costs can reconcile consumption and stock returns?'. *Journal of Political Economy* **107**, 969–997.

Lynch, A. W. and S. Tan (2004), 'Explaining the magnitude of liquidity premia: The roles of return predictability, wealth shocks and state-dependent transaction costs'. Working Paper, New York University.

Macey, J. and M. O'Hara (2005), 'Down and out in the stock market: The law and economics of the delisting process'. Working Paper, Cornell University.

Madhavan, A. (2000), 'Market microstructure: A survey'. *Journal of Financial Markets* **3**, 205–258.

Madrigal, V. (1996), 'Non-fundamental speculation'. *The Journal of Finance* **51**, 553–578.

Maher, J. M. (1976), 'Discounts for lack of marketability for closely held business interests'. *Taxes* **xx**, 562–571.

Manzler, D. (2004), 'Liquidity, liquidity risk and the closed-end fund discount'. Working Paper, University of Cincinnati.

Markowitz, H. (1952), 'Portfolio selection'. *Journal of Finance* **7**, 77–91.

Marshall, B. R. (2005), 'Liquidity and Stock Returns: Evidence from a pure order-driven market using a new liquidity proxy'. Working Paper, Massey University, New Zealand.

Martinez, M. L., B. Nieto, G. Rubio, and M. Tapia (2005), 'Asset pricing and systematic liquidity risk: An empirical investigation of the Spanish stock market'. *International Review of Economics and Finance* **14**, 81–103.

Mendelson, H. and T. Tunca (2004), 'Strategic trading, liquidity and information acquisition'. *Review of Financial Studies* **17**, 295–337.

Mendelson, H. (1982), 'Market behavior in a clearing house'. *Econometrica* **50**, 1505–1524.

Merton, R. C. (1987), 'A simple model of capital market equilibrium with incomplete information'. *Journal of Finance* **42**, 483–510.

Mossin, J. (1966), 'Equilibrium in a capital asset market'. *Econometrica* **35**, 768–783.

Muscarella, C. J. and M. S. Piwowar (2001), 'Market microstructure and securities values: Evidence from the Paris bourse'. *Journal of Financial Markets* **4**, 209–229.

Nguyen, D., S. Mishra, and A. J. Prakash (2005), 'On compensation for illiquidity in asset pricing: An empirical evaluation using three-factor model and three-moment CAPM'. Working Paper, Florida International University.

Novy-Marx, R. (2005), 'The excess returns to illiquidity'. Working Paper, University of Chicago.

Ofek, E., M. Richardson, and R. F. Whitelaw (2004), 'Limited arbitrage and short-sales restrictions: Evidence from the options markets'. *Journal of Financial Economics*. Forthcoming.

O'Hara, M. (1995), *Market Microstructure Theory*. Blackwell Publishers, Cambridge, MA.

O'Hara, M. (2003), 'Presidential address: Liquidity and price discovery'. *Journal of Finance* **58**, 1335–1354.

Pastor, L. and R. Stambaugh (2003), 'Liquidity risk and expected stock returns'. *Journal of Political Economy* **111**, 642–685.

Pratt, S. (2003), 'Business Valuation Update 9'.

Livingston, M. and L. Zhou (2002), 'The impact of Rule 144A debt offerings upon bond yields and underwriter fees'. *Financial Management* **xx**, 5–27.

Loderer, C. and L. Roth (2005), 'The pricing discount for limited liquidity: Evidence from SWX Swiss Exchange and the Nasdaq'. *Journal of Empirical Finance* **12**, 239–268.

Longstaff, F. A. (2001), 'Optimal portfolio choice and the valuation of illiquid securities'. *Review of Financial Studies* **14**, 407–431.

Longstaff, F. A. (2004), 'The flight-to-liquidity premium in U.S. Treasury bond prices'. *Journal of Business*. Forthcoming.

Longstaff, F. (1995), 'How much can marketability affect security values?'. *The Journal of Finance* **50**, 1767–1774.

Lo, A. W., H. Mamaysky, and J. Wang (2004), 'Asset prices and trading volume under fixed transaction costs'. *Journal of Political Economy* **112**, 1054–1090.

Luttmer, E. G. (1996), 'Asset pricing in economies with frictions'. *Econometrica* **64**, 1439–1467.

Luttmer, E. G. (1999), 'What level of fixed costs can reconcile consumption and stock returns?'. *Journal of Political Economy* **107**, 969–997.

Lynch, A. W. and S. Tan (2004), 'Explaining the magnitude of liquidity premia: The roles of return predictability, wealth shocks and state-dependent transaction costs'. Working Paper, New York University.

Macey, J. and M. O'Hara (2005), 'Down and out in the stock market: The law and economics of the delisting process'. Working Paper, Cornell University.

Madhavan, A. (2000), 'Market microstructure: A survey'. *Journal of Financial Markets* **3**, 205–258.

Madrigal, V. (1996), 'Non-fundamental speculation'. *The Journal of Finance* **51**, 553–578.

Maher, J. M. (1976), 'Discounts for lack of marketability for closely held business interests'. *Taxes* **xx**, 562–571.

Manzler, D. (2004), 'Liquidity, liquidity risk and the closed-end fund discount'. Working Paper, University of Cincinnati.

Markowitz, H. (1952), 'Portfolio selection'. *Journal of Finance* **7**, 77–91.

Marshall, B. R. (2005), 'Liquidity and Stock Returns: Evidence from a pure order-driven market using a new liquidity proxy'. Working Paper, Massey University, New Zealand.

Martinez, M. L., B. Nieto, G. Rubio, and M. Tapia (2005), 'Asset pricing and systematic liquidity risk: An empirical investigation of the Spanish stock market'. *International Review of Economics and Finance* **14**, 81–103.

Mendelson, H. and T. Tunca (2004), 'Strategic trading, liquidity and information acquisition'. *Review of Financial Studies* **17**, 295–337.

Mendelson, H. (1982), 'Market behavior in a clearing house'. *Econometrica* **50**, 1505–1524.

Merton, R. C. (1987), 'A simple model of capital market equilibrium with incomplete information'. *Journal of Finance* **42**, 483–510.

Mossin, J. (1966), 'Equilibrium in a capital asset market'. *Econometrica* **35**, 768–783.

Muscarella, C. J. and M. S. Piwowar (2001), 'Market microstructure and securities values: Evidence from the Paris bourse'. *Journal of Financial Markets* **4**, 209–229.

Nguyen, D., S. Mishra, and A. J. Prakash (2005), 'On compensation for illiquidity in asset pricing: An empirical evaluation using three-factor model and three-moment CAPM'. Working Paper, Florida International University.

Novy-Marx, R. (2005), 'The excess returns to illiquidity'. Working Paper, University of Chicago.

Ofek, E., M. Richardson, and R. F. Whitelaw (2004), 'Limited arbitrage and short-sales restrictions: Evidence from the options markets'. *Journal of Financial Economics*. Forthcoming.

O'Hara, M. (1995), *Market Microstructure Theory*. Blackwell Publishers, Cambridge, MA.

O'Hara, M. (2003), 'Presidential address: Liquidity and price discovery'. *Journal of Finance* **58**, 1335–1354.

Pastor, L. and R. Stambaugh (2003), 'Liquidity risk and expected stock returns'. *Journal of Political Economy* **111**, 642–685.

Pratt, S. (2003), 'Business Valuation Update 9'.

Pritsker, M. (2003), 'Large investors: Implications for equilibrium asset returns, shock absorption, and liquidity'. *Mimeo, Board of Governors of the Federal Reserve System.*

Rabinovitch, R., A. C. Silva, and R. Susmel (2003), 'Returns on ADRs and arbitrage in emerging markets'. *Emerging Markets Review* **4**, 225–247.

Reinganum, M. R. (1981), 'Misspecification of capital asset pricing: Empirical anomalies based on earnings yields and market values'. *Journal of Financial Economics* **9**, 127–147.

Reinganum, M. R. (1990), 'Market microstructure and asset pricing'. *Journal of Financial Economics* **28**, 127–147.

Roll, R. (1985), 'A simple implicit measure of the effective bid-ask spread in an efficient market'. *Journal of Finance* **39**, 1127–1139.

Ross, S. A. (1989), 'Information and volatility: The no-arbitrage martingale approach to timing and resolution irrelevancy'. *Journal of Finance* **44**, 1–17.

Rouwenhorst, K. G. (1999), 'Local return factors and turnover in emerging stock markets'. *Journal of Finance* **54**, 1439–1464.

Sadka, R. (2003), 'Liquidity risk and asset pricing'. Working Paper, University of Washington.

Sharpe, W. (1964), 'Capital asset prices: A theory of capital market equilibrium under conditions of risk'. *Journal of Finance* **19**, 425–442.

Silber, W. L. (1975), 'Thinness in capital markets: The case of the Tel Aviv stock exchange'. *Journal of Financial and Quantitative Analysis* **10**, 129–142.

Silber, W. L. (1991), 'Discounts on restricted stock: The impact of illiquidity on stock prices'. *Financial Analysts Journal* **47**, 60–64.

Solberg, T. A. (1979), 'Valuing restricted securities: What factors do the courts and the service look for?'. *Journal of Taxation* **xx**, 150–154.

Spiegel, M. and X. Wang (2005), 'Cross-sectional variation in stock returns: Liquidity and idiosyncratic risk'. Working Paper, Yale University.

Stoll, H. R. and R. H. Whaley (1983), 'Transaction costs and the small firm effect'. *Journal of Financial Economics* **12**, 57–79.

Stoll, H. R. (1978b), 'The pricing of security dealers services: An empirical study of Nasdaq stocks'. *Journal of Finance* **33**, 1153–1172.

Stoll, H. (1978a), 'The supply of dealer services in securities markets'. *Journal of Finance* **33**, 1133–1151.

Strebulaev, I. A. (2002), 'Many faces of liquidity and asset pricing: Evidence from the U.S. Treasury securities market'. Working Paper, Stanford University.

Swan, P. L. and J. J. Westerholm (2002), 'Asset prices and liquidity: The impact of endogenous trading'. Working Paper, University of New South Wales.

Trout, R. R. (1977), 'Estimation of the discount associated with the transfer of restricted securities'. *Taxes* **xx**, 381–385.

Vayanos, D. and J.-L. Vila (1999), 'Equilibrium interest rate and liquidity premium with transaction costs'. *Economic Theory* **13**, 509–539.

Vayanos, D. and T. Wang (2002), 'Search and endogenous concentration of liquidity in asset markets'. Working Paper, MIT.

Vayanos, D. and P.-O. Weill (2005), 'A search-based theory of the on the-run phenomenon'. Working Paper, LSE.

Vayanos, D. (1998), 'Transaction costs and asset prices: A dynamic equilibrium model'. *Review of Financial Studies* **11**, 1–58.

Vayanos, D. (2001), 'Strategic trading in a dynamic noisy market'. *The Journal of Finance* **56**, 131–171.

Vayanos, D. (2004), 'Flight to quality, flight to liquidity and the pricing of risk'. Working Paper, LSE.

Wang, J. (1993), 'A model of intertemporal asset prices under asymmetric information'. *Review of Economic Studies* **60**, 249–282.

Wang, J. (1994), 'A model of competitive stock trading volume'. *Journal of Political Economy* **102**, 127–168.

Warga, A. (1992), 'Bond returns, liquidity, and missing data'. *Journal of Financial and Quantitative Analysis* **27**, 605–617.

Weill, P.-O. (2002), 'The liquidity premium in a dynamic bargaining market'. Working Paper, Stanford University.

Weill, P.-O. (2003), 'Leaning against the wind'. Working Paper, Stanford University.